Object-choice

Object-choice
(All you need is love ...)

On mating strategies
&
a fragment of a Freud biography

———————◆———————

k l a u s   t h e w e l e i t

Translated by Malcolm Green

VERSO

London · New York

First published as *Objektwahl (All You Need Is Love)* 1990
© Stroemfeld/Roter Stern
© This edition Verso 1994
Translation © Malcolm R. Green 1994
All rights reserved

Verso
UK: 6 Meard Street, London W1V 3HR
USA: 29 West 35th Street, New York, NY 10001-2291

Verso is the imprint of New Left Books

ISBN 978-0-86091-642-0

British Library Cataloguing in Publication Data
A catalogue record for this book is available from the British Library

Library of Congress Cataloging-in-Publication Data
A catalogue record for this book is available from the Library of Congress

Typeset by Solidus (Bristol) Limited

Contents

Translator's Note

Correspondence between Freud, C.G. and Emma Jung is taken from *Sigmund Freud–C.G. Jung: Briefwechsel*, Frankfurt am Main 1974. All other Freud correspondence is taken from Sigmund Freud, *Briefe 1873–1939*, ed. and introduced by Ernst Freud, Frankfurt am Main 1968. Ernst Freud's introduction to this volume is also quoted. The excerpts from Freud's 'On Narcissism: An Introduction' are taken from *The Complete Psychological Works of Sigmund Freud*, trans. and ed. James Strachey, Standard Edition vol. 14, London 1957, pp. 90, 78, 88–90. Minor alterations have been made where the present text made this necessary.

Other source details are as follows. The quotation from Greil Marcus on p. 3 is from *Lipstick Traces: A Secret History of the Twentieth Century*, London 1990, p. 431. Theweleit's *Male Fantasies*, cited on p. 12, is available in a two-volume English edition: *Vol. 1. Women, Floods, Bodies, History*, trans. S. Conway with E. Carter and C. Turner, Cambridge 1987; *Vol. 2. Psychoanalysing the White Terror*, trans. E. Carter and C. Turner, Cambridge 1989. The Hitchcock quote on p. 21 is from Donald Spoto, *The Life of Alfred Hitchcock: The Dark Side of Genius*, London 1983, p. 65. The quotes from Hannah Arendt's biography (relating to the relationship with Heidegger) on pp. 28 and 29 are from Elisabeth Young-Bruehl, *Hannah Arendt: For Love of the World*, New Haven, Conn. 1982, pp. 50 and 53–4 respectively. The quote from Arendt on p. 29 is taken from 'What is Existenz Philosophy?', *Partisan Review*, 8 (1), Winter 1946, pp. 34–56. Sara Paretsky's *Burn Marks*, cited on p. 35, was published in London in 1991. The July 1933 letter from Céline to Cillie Pam (addressed as 'N') which appears on p. 37 is taken from *Cahiers Céline 5: Lettres à des amies*, selected and ed. Colin W. Nettelbeck, Paris 1979, p. 106. The quotes from Frank J. Sulloway on pp. 44 and 45 are from *Freud: Biologist of the Mind. Beyond the Psychoanalytic Legend*, London 1979, pp. 56–7. The quotes from Ernest Jones on pp. 57 and 58 are from *The Life and Works of Sigmund Freud*, ed. and abridged by Lionel Trilling and Steven Marcus, Harmondsworth 1976, p. 474. The quote from Mann's diaries on p. 89 is from *Thomas Mann, Tagebücher 28.5.1946–31.12.1948*, ed. Inge Jens, Frankfurt am Main 1989. H.D.'s *Tribute to Freud*, cited on p. 91, was published in New York in 1956. The quotes on pp. 93 and 94 from Elisabeth Young-Bruehl (regarding Anna Freud's relationship with Dorothy Burlingham) are taken from *Anna Freud: A Biography*, New York 1988, pp. 135 and 192 respectively. The Hirsch source cited on p. 98 is *The Mother–Daughter Plot: Narrative, Psychoanalysis, Feminism*, Bloomington, Ind. 1989. The 'Beatles' quote on p. 109 is taken from Hunter Davies, *The Beatles: The Authorised Biography*, London 1968, p. 157. Finally, the Heine poem on p. 111, stanza no. 6 of 'New Spring', is the translation by Hal Draper in *The Complete Poems of Heinrich Heine*, Oxford 1982, p. 316.

My thanks to Justin Dyer for his valuable help in tracing source material for this edition.

If I was a little bird
with two little car wings,
I'd fly straight to you.*
    (VLADO KRISTL, 'Death to the Spectator')

---

*A paraphrase of a famous German folk song expressing longing. (Trans.)

* * *

Initially this was a talk for an interdisciplinary series of lectures entitled 'Psychoanalysis and the Present' held at Frankfurt University, and given at the invitation of Christa Rohde-Dachser, Institut für Psychoanalyse, on 17 January 1990. Then repeated the day after in Berlin, in the Georg-Kolbe-Museum, at the invitation of Edelgard Abenstein, in connection with the exhibitions on women in the 20th century put on by various Berlin museums. Talk, revised and extended version.

Having recently spent a couple of months in Arcadia (as parts of America used to be named on early European maps), where I had the chance to get a whiff of American academia in New England, ditto our children of New England schools and my wife of whatever took her fancy – i.e. *life* came first – neither volumes 2 or 3 of the *Book of Kings** have advanced sufficiently to go to press.

This seemed to have more or less the right format to prevent the gap between volume 1 and the rest from growing any larger. After all, I also believe (readers, listeners, my publisher) that one mustn't always hide *everything* in-between 1003 pages.

Object-choice is taken largely from the typescripts for volume 3 on Freud, which is in progress. The present book can be placed on the bookshelf next to it, if and when volume 3 appears, as *vol. 3a*.

I would like to thank Christian Schaeffer, Monika Theweleit-Kubale, Margret Berger and Martin Langbein, who made themselves available during the book's genesis this summer as readers

---

*Volume 1 of the *Book of Kings* (*Buch der Könige*) appeared in German in 1988 (Frankfurt am Main). Entitled *Orpheus and Eurydice*, it revolves around the Orpheus myth as one of male artistic production at the cost of medial women (Euridyces) skilled in technical appliances, and includes studies of, among others, the poets Gottfried Benn and Else Lasker-Schüler, Brecht, Hamsun and Rilke, all of whom receive mentions or more in the present volume. Volumes 2 to 4 will centre on the figures of Benn, Freud and Céline respectively (Trans.)

and helpers, and for their corrections, material, suggestions, rejections and their general approval (the greatest help when one's in a hurry).

There are no pictures to this text; this is connected with a sensible rule from the Old Testament, the *ban on images* of the *object*, the first commandment of LOVE (and naturally misunderstood there, because it's applied solely to love for the Lord). But hopefully it has *sounds*.

In America one could see that the vinyl record, that old beauty, is dying. For most record stores it has already died. This book is dedicated to everyone whose life and love (also) play(ed) on vinyl discs, *to the last Ptolemaeans*. The next plays on others.

Freiburg, 21 August 1990

The headings on the various pages (column titles) are from songs by:
Pp. 2 f. (Jimi Hendrix) / 4 ff. (Bob Dylan) / 7 f. (Hendrix) / 9 f. (The Beatles) / 11 f. (Prince) / 13 f. (The Rolling Stones) / 15 ff. (Stones) / 19 f. (Prince) / 21 f. (Hendrix) / 23 f. (Wyatt Day) / 25 f. (The Kinks) / 27 (Ray Charles) / 28 ff. (Hendrix) / 32 ff. (Beatles) / 36 (Ray Charles) / 37 (Prince) / 38 f. (Beatles) / 40 f. (Stones) / 42 f. (Beatles) / 44 ff. (Ray Charles) / 48 ff. (Barry Mann) / 52 (Stones) / 53 (Beatles) / 54 ff. (Nico & Velvet Underground) / 58 ff. (Dylan) / 61 ff. (Hendrix) / 65 f. (Dylan) / 67 f. (Stones) / 69 ff. (Nico & Velvet Underground) / 76 f. (Ray Charles) / 78 f. (Hendrix) / 80 f. (J.J. Cale) / 82 ff. (Ray Charles) / 85 ff. (Hendrix) / 89 (Dylan) / 90 f. (Leonard Cohen) / 92 f. (Dylan) / 94 f. (Beatles) / 96 ff. (Hendrix) / 99 (Dylan) / 100 f. (Hendrix).

The song titles in the text are from Lennon/McCartney (pp. 10, 21), Hendrix (pp. 18, 33), Harrison (p. 41) and Prince (p. 99). The three lines of poetry on p. 100 are from Vlado Kristl.

Object-choice

When we hear about the ways people marry, we, fully automated children of the age of liberated love, also think of the ways people love. Ways of marrying, ways of loving:

– when, on the 25 June 1967, right in the middle of the 'Summer of Love',* the BBC in London made the first satellite link-up for a live television transmission from one side of the planet to the other (3 American, 1 Russian satellites; 300 cameras in 42 locations around the world; each country providing a *special contribution*: the West Germans Bayreuth/Wagner), it went almost without saying that the bosses of the British Broadcasting Corporation did not search in their own studios for the wedding music to the tele-communications marriage of the antipodean hemispheres; they took their cameras to EMI & the Beatles, and John Lennon brought the world-unifying anthem ALL YOU NEED IS LOVE, introduced by a fanfare from the 'Marseillaise', to the entire globe, now finally united McLuhan fashion. *OUR WORLD*, the pro-gramme was called.

Marseillaises, 1789 ff., 1967, aware that they were heralding new times. All you need is love – what else.

For the broadcasting industry, for the marriage industry, for all the means of cosmically embracing the world, for philosophy, religions, for the sciences of humanity as well as for bearing the daily workload and for shopping in the supermarket – all you need is. Anyone who is relaxed and well-balanced and is properly (cordlessly) linked up also has time, money and freedom, and lives

---

*Behind the shelter in the middle of the roundabout, as the pop singers put it ...

1

and loves with the right people; everything arrives of its own accord where LOVE is.*

For the last twenty or thirty years the West has been out searching for this LOVE, and broadcasting this search twenty-four hours a day around the globe; so much so that even the normally immovable East began to open its walls and gateways, to cast itself into the longing arms of West-love.

West-love . . . this is the news, the glad tidings of this half of the century – and it was received loud and clear; if not here, then elsewhere.**

In the WEST, from where the message is broadcast, 'love' is not regarded that highly by enlightened Westerners as a way of conducting one's life. Although the majority believe that one way or another *All you need is Love*, there is relatively little faith that one will actually find or receive 'the love' that one needs. What counts here is experience, not some belief: love is an unloved feeling.

Happiness is sought elsewhere, in work, in relationships at work, in other social ties, in commodities, on the real estate market, in cultural settings, in the production of art or children, in self-improvement, in peace and unpeaceful movements, in pills one pops: elsewhere. LOVE here is a waste- or by-product, turns up in passing, remains a while and is then allowed to move on.

For much of the past and in most societies, the ways people marry have nothing to do with the ways they love. Now and then there have been a few oases in history, periods of time, places,

---

*The song was written specially for the show. 'We had been told we'd be seen recording it by the whole world at the same time. So we had one message for the world – "Love". We need more love in the world. It's a period in history that needs love.' (Paul McCartney on 22 July 1967 in an interview with the *New Musical Express*.)

**In January 1990 television showed more shots from the Land of the East, this time Bulgaria, Sofia. People out on the streets with 'All You Need Is Love' on their banners and coming out of the speakers. (Erich Brinkmann and Bernd Walz told me this after the lecture in West Berlin.)

where so-called marriage for love was of importance to a small number of people. Its emergence in our civilization is closely linked to the medium of writing, with letters which emancipate themselves from the texts of the Bible and encode particular areas captured from the public realm with the words 'woman' and 'love'. 'Love' was first and foremost a concern of literature, at several places in Southern France in the 9th and 12th centuries, in Italy around 1300, once again in France and Italy after 1500, in England up to around 1600, in Germany only shortly before 1800. Ovid made an important attempt around the year zero. **It was a turning point in history where history refused to turn** (as Greil Marcus noted of Paris, May '68). A lovely sentence, which fits numerous turning points.

'Love' as a topic; love as a generator of ways of writing, of types of text, love as a tragic theme and as a type of text 'encoded with death': for obviously people carried on marrying according to completely different criteria than that a man and a woman were in love. Only in the 20th century, after the First World War, after the removal of the majority of militaristic-monarchic systems, as love passed from the books on to screens and vinyl (or: after America's media kiss on Europe's tired young lips), has there been something like a mass experiment with love-marriages; marriages based on feelings, even in those social strata that have never been able to afford this luxury because of the sheer exhaustion and fatigue caused by excessively hard work, inadequate food and the over-crowding of the available living space. Love was perhaps a song, or it was brought to life by a couple after their wedding.

Also the first ever love-marriages for many women from various strata; after WW1 not only the right to elect (men to parliaments) was granted ... but also 'love-choice' as a new freedom for daughters (some of whom, especially Americans, chose another daughter as mate). However, the universal spirit in its wisdom – trench warfare – had the foresight at the same time to plant the sting of a surplus of women in these new possibilities, so allowing *men* to be choosy. I will never grasp how one can be in love with Hegelian dialectic.

Now all my fathers, they've gone down . . .

*

All you need is Love– a farmer of the last four centuries would have replied: what he *needs* is a good working wife who will give birth to sturdy children, keeps an eye on the purse and doesn't spoil the food. Earlier the serfs received the woman the landlords gave or allowed them.

A prince would have answered: he needs a young daughter from another powerful principality; a woman who brings troops and money in her train, guarantees an increase in power and who must naturally also bear heirs to the throne, sons.

A merchant's son from one of the business enterprises of the 19th century could not (and in most cases would not) marry anyone but the daughter of another firm, with the aim of financial fusions, generating further firms and giving birth to Peter Petersen, Jr, III.

Workers in the 19th century married women who (if possible) could and wanted to sew, cook, get hold of firewood, keep the home free of vermin and the bailiff from the door, etc., not to mention the necessary skills in the case of hunger and cold. More often than not, the bride and groom had shared the same premises (lodgers and lodgings). Marriages were hastened or decided by pregnancy: object-choice on the basis of living under the same roof (a very common way of finding a partner in all centuries and in several classes); now of renewed importance in student and other flat-sharing milieux.

I am not speaking here of the ability to take the blows, nor of the actual forms of sexuality, which only become important after marriage, not in the *choice* of marriage partner.

There are other ways of marrying which are no less familiar than these: in the papers the international 'news in brief' regularly reports double weddings in India, for instance, in which the wrong couples were married. Of course, the brides and grooms did not know one another beforehand. We smile, but it wasn't very different here: as a rule the people who were marked out for marriage were not asked.

In these types of marriage, 'the woman' (a daughter) is either

4

part of the paternal economy, bringing money or taking some of it away, creating coalitions and power and business ties; or is part and parcel of her husband's economic needs; she must restore his energies for work, help him get by or climb the ranks, keep the children in the right order (proper religion, sphincter control), until they are old enough to be taken from her for further dressing by a male social institution. She has to represent her husband's power at the appropriate social level. She is there to fulfil his sexual, genealogical and other needs.

Sometimes sexual fidelity is required, and sometimes not; that all depends on the kind of economy, the regulation of inheritances, on living conditions, the organization of public life and so on.

The daughter's exclusion from her kin/family and her removal to another whose name she adopts (whereby certain contracts are signed and goods bartered, which the daughter has nothing to do with) is the foundation of the patriarchal system of family formation, from the Old Testament to the present day.*

So, historically, the concept 'marital forms' is synonymous with procedures for trading daughters, while excluding the daughters' sexuality.

'*Do you love me?*' – '*Do I WHAT?*' (Dialogue between two parents, older psycho-class, Jewish, in a Broadway musical as a daughter, younger psycho-class, says she wants to marry for 'love' a different man from the one chosen for her.)

All you need is a daughter (later wife) who can, or gives the impression that she can, do all that is necessary or desirable according to the conditions of male business, male politics and the male politics of procreation. Hence marrying according to economic, religious or ethnic rules, to relevant social geography, for political advantage; no daughters from another village, or *only* from

---

*This is described very nicely in Lynda Boose's 'The Father's House and the Daughter in It: The Structures of Western Culture's Daughter–Father-Relationship', in Lynda Boose & Betty S. Flowers, eds, *Daughters & Fathers*, Baltimore, Maryland 1989.

another village; none of a different religion; none from another class, or *only* from another class (for marriages of alliance or those intended for social advancement); none from a different trade, with a different dialect . . . and the rest of the repertoire of racism.

*

It is no coincidence that only at the beginning of the 20th century marriage did someone hit on the idea of studying marriage from the perspective of the love-choice; love-choice above all; an affect which follows psychic laws. As far as I can see, Freud is the first theoretician in history who attempts to link forms of marriage with forms of being in love, with ways of loving in which the paternal economy does not play a decisive role. (As we shall see, it does play a role after all; but Freud makes considerable alterations to it.)

Combining love & marriage transgresses the socio-economic rules, one could also say, economic reason. For this, as with all relevant transgressions against society, a certain state is required, a state of intoxication, of exquisite madness, which generates the energy necessary to abandon the traditional bed-rock of behaviour and makes imminent punishment seem insignificant. The presumably first theoretician of love as a ground for marriage does not hesitate to place this feeling, to which he will pay considerable attention, in the proximity of mental illness as a major deviation from normality.

Love-marriage is a kind of madness, says Freud. A madness, however, which follows certain rules. The basic rules can be put quite simply: here, instead of the normal understanding of reality according to specific demands of the reality principle, there is a misperception (an impairment of the ego, says Freud), a fundamental misperception of the love-object, the main characteristic of which is an excessive overvaluation of the loved object, especially a sexual overvaluation, accompanied by its idealization. Subsequently the person who misperceives identifies with this overvalued, misperceived object – or more precisely this *female* object, because basically we are speaking of a male procedure. Women, says Freud, have only a limited capacity for this fundamental misperception called 'love'; 'total object-love', as he puts it in 'On Narcissism', 1914, is not found among them.

This is not a simply 'anti-female' statement if one formulates it in a way that is tacitly implied by Freud: women are slightly less *mad* than men, for they are more useful (and later we shall see for what).

The people he knows, says Freud, mainly fall in love in two ways: according to the attachment (anaclytic) model and according to the narcissistic model. Love in the *attachment model* is based on the person who provided the first experiences of satisfaction. Generally this is the mother who held and fed the child.

The *narcissistic model* describes those adults whose love-object is derived not from the example of their mothers, but rather from their own selves. Quite evidently they look to themselves as love-objects, says Freud, who refers to this behaviour as a *disorder* in the development of the libido.

He divides the two models (while mentioning possible exceptions and hybrid forms) roughly between the two sexes. Men tend to love according to the attachment model, women according to the 'narcissistic' one.

Jumping ahead slightly, I should add that in his text on narcissism Freud names four types of female object-choice, which, on closer inspection, all amount to being of particular benefit to the man with whom they are associated. I say 'the man' here deliberately, because I hope to show that Freud himself is this man. He devises a model of female love-choices which is tailored to the kinds of women with whom he was associated in the course of his private and institutional life. They are patients; they are women who became psychoanalysts under him; they are his wife and his sisters; and they are his daughters for whose psycho-sexual development Freud in 1914 devises this model (and it is his daughter Anna who will later be a match for this model). For each of these categories of women there is a specific sort of satisfaction resulting from the type of object-choice foreseen for them; and every type of choice contains something that is of benefit to Freud's life work, for the foundation and maintenance of the psychoanalytic state.

I think I have said enough now to plant the idea that even Freud's forms of object-choice have something to do with strategies (and not merely with mothers or 'narcissistic' self-love).

After a while I shall turn to Freud's own marriage – his love-choice, underlined by fifteen hundred love letters.

Was it love? And if so, which kind?

* * *

I. Lexicon of love

Object-choice according to the attachment model.

When looking for confirmation of Freud's categories in their own experience, most people will probably come up with object-choices of the attachment type: men who always fall in love with the same 'type' of woman ('mothers'?); women who are always seen with the same type of man (in various versions – 'fathers'?). Some of them have married or are otherwise liaised, for the second or third time, with partners who have such blatant physical similarities with their own mother or father that it would be difficult to maintain that this had played no part in their object-choice. It is not even necessary to know the parents to see this. Freud's basic assumption about this kind of love-choice – the desire to have something *back*, which had once existed – is at least partly involved in the way all these men and women keep falling in love with the same brown eyes, the same slender gait, the same curve of the lips, the same cheekbones and hips.

This *getting* back is not, however, easy, as can be seen from the tendency to form a sequence of partners that is inherent in the description of this type of object-choice. The reason for this is probably that the loved ones who are chosen because they are supposed to bring something *back* are insufficiently similar to the person who provides the model; or are sufficiently similar but develop too much life of their own. The majority of real women will neither wish nor be able to satisfy the demands of *substituting* – physically, emotionally – for certain characteristics of the man's mother; the same applies to the men who are elected to replace certain daughters' fathers. There appears to be a tendency towards 'error and disillusionment' in these relationships – you are not at all like 'my mother'/'my father' – I don't even want to be like 'your mother'/'your father' – you disappoint me – no, you simply don't understand me.... A major form of the object-choice which Freud proposes would seem to be one in which 'love' is easily kindled, but has the greatest difficulties in growing and enduring.

There can be no doubt that strong affect plays a role in this choice. Some men I know recognize the connection between their loved one and certain features of their mother; it fills them with distrust. Nevertheless they continue to be in love, or fall in love with a woman of the same type. Awareness of a symptom, awareness of the origins and significance of a symptom, does not remove it, as Freud says. Evidently the affective power which asserts itself is greater than the power of self-critical perception, in which the fear that the familiar *failure* might repeat itself is lurking in the background.

> The long and winding road
> That leads to your door
> Will never disappear,
> I've seen that road before,
> It always leads me here,
> Leads me to your door.

Other people marry a man or a woman whose physical constitution differs appreciably from that of their father or mother. That does not necessarily mean that this has nothing to do with 'attachment'; rather the choice was not made on the basis of some *resemblance* with the father or mother.

Presumably the relationship with the parent of the same sex plays a role in this form of object-choice. For a man, for example, to love a woman who does *not* resemble his mother means that he is not repeating his father, is making a different choice, loving in a different way – perhaps he will even *become* different (to his father). Accordingly the attachment to one parent sometimes appears in the form of an avoidance of visible attachment. Thus one can safely place the love-choice of the attachment type with the choice based on rejection. A man or woman is loved because of the greatest possible dissimilarity to the parent of the opposite sex. But this, too, can lead to the long and winding road (and always to the same door ...).

As ever, Freud writes about things which happen.

Whether they actually happen in the way Freud presents them is another question. In love-choices of the attachment type it is not certain, for instance, whether the chooser wishes to *regain a pleasure* that once came from his mother (in Freud's eyes the main affect in such a choice). A number of people I know who make attachment love-choices speak of anything but loving or caring mothers; more the opposite, of mothers who did not look after them, who were often away and pursued other matters. So would 'loving' here imply 'loving' women in the image of a mother who was not affectionate? And what function could the loved one, whom they loved in attachment to this mother, have for them?

Self-punishment through a woman who resembles an *unloved* mother? (To ease guilt feelings, say, which originate in suppressed rage at the mother?)

Do they want to be the father in a relationship in which they teach a woman who accords with the image of an unloved mother how to be a 'proper' mother (e.g. to one's own children)?

Do they want to punish their own wives in place of their mothers, who are out of reach of their revenge, were always out of reach?

A number of reasons are conceivable besides those given by Freud; in particular a love-choice based on un-pleasure affects. It is equally probable, however, that the choice is often triggered by a bundle of affects consisting in part of *contradictory* affects.

A man who had been abandoned by his mother at the age of three (she jumped from the top of a house) falls in love with a woman who has just left her three-year-old daughter, and she falls in love with him, the adult who had been abandoned at the age of three. Both find *again* what they did not wish to keep, or what *she* did not wish to keep: object-choice stemming from interlocking attachments (with an unhappy end). There is a good deal of history contained in some love stories, more than and different from the wish to regain the love in the womb or the flow of milk and caresses.

... more than I hate to see U sad.

*

Another elaboration of the Freudian construct of 'attachment love' arises more or less as a matter of course. It is not a primarily male choice, as Freud defines it. There are no fewer women who choose their men according to what a father had once been to them (positively or negatively) than men who 'turn back to their mothers'. From this can be concluded that the pleasure to which one is attached, wants to have back, is not necessarily just the pleasure received from one's mother as an infant (which has something very irretrievable about it). Love of the attachment type is, in Freud's construct, a bit like being in love with the moon (which, for all its beauty, is difficult to touch).

In a moment we shall see whether it is at all appropriate simply to place mothers (or fathers; which Freud did not do) in the construct of attachment: I am thinking here of siblings, whose reciprocal relations still only play a very subordinate role in Freudian psychoanalysis.

The 'comrade's sister' or 'best friend's brother'.

During the first half of this century, the male type whom I have termed the 'soldierly male' mainly married the sister of a comrade, if possible the sister of his 'best friend' (the female doppelganger of his best friend), so basically not a woman at all.

In *Male Fantasies* I described the strongest affect in this choice as the urge to avoid: avoidance of a possibly erotic, demanding woman, a woman with 'experience' and desires. Coming from the family of a dear, 'upright' friend acts like a seal of approval and purity; the seal of not-being-a-tart, stuck on by the brother-state. Here a *name* is being married, the name of another *man*. It guarantees that she will not flood him with emotions which might dissolve his physicality, with its hard-earned armour; and the brother guarantees her 'obedience'. This form of marriage can be classified under the defence mechanisms. 'The woman' in her is a physical-psychical security system warding off feared forms of life; and as such she receives the ring. And this marriage is intended to produce not children, but rather new comrades, soldiers. Object-choice *white nurse/sister.*

12

If this form of object-choice contains anything of the attachment type, the writings of these men reveal that it is attachment to the physical constitution of a sister who in most cases is slightly older. By identifying with one's 'friend', this choice of marital partner can allow the hidden satisfaction of incestuous desires. But what does 'hidden' mean here? Previously I viewed this type of marriage as a variation of the 'virgin marriage'; that was probably naïve. Statistical probability suggests that many of these sisters were the object of nocturnal attacks by family fathers or these brothers themselves; so the marital form 'comrade's sister' can also be viewed as an agency for the discreet exchange of deflowered sisters between families. Both sides knew that no one from *outside the family* was being considered as husband; a safety catch in more than one respect.

This man does not manage to get as far as his mother as 'object', and doesn't get beyond his sister; she demarcates the *boundary* of possible object-choices.

What does that mean – he does not get as far as his mother? It means that this type of man is incapable of an 'object-choice' in the Freudian sense because he does not reach the state of a psychically grounded distinction between subject and object. He remains tied to his mother's body in a symbiotic state that is experienced negatively and is never adequately dissolved. And for precisely this reason the mother becomes neither an 'object' nor the model for a possible choice. I have termed this type of person the 'not-fully-born-man', who has a muscular 'ego' (body armour) as the result of inflicted pain, punishments and drill, and whose physical attempts at releasing tensions should be viewed as processes aimed not at producing pleasure, but rather at self-preservation.

'Maintenance mechanisms' – Margaret Mahler's description for certain infants whose development has been arrested. This man's object-choice can be categorized as a maintenance mechanism. Although it is an affect, indeed a strong one, it is not one of being in love or love. In a sense this kind of partner choice does not even belong in a consideration of forms of love; against this, sociologically and statistically, it was one of the most widespread forms of marriage in Germany till around 1950. One cannot simply disregard it, but should note that until very recently the majority of marriages have been the result of anything but love. It is just that the marital form adopted by these soldierly males of the 20th century, whose bodies are marked by the pain principle, is dictated no longer by economic or corresponding social reasons, but to a large extent by *psychical* ones. At the historical moment that seemed to open up the possibility of 'love-marriages' to many, the majority of men reacted first of all with a protective mechanism, physically incapable of dealing with freer women and freer forms of eroticism. They set up something like Siegfried Lines and Atlantic Walls on their own bodies, fortifications against the invasions.

With their muscular sensors, they detected any deviations from the Hitler-Germanic norm during the thirties and forties with a certainty that scarcely missed a needle in a haystack if previously it had been touched by Jewish hand. For them 'Jewish' was above all a sexual word (= *they dissolve our bodies*); then a political word (= *they dissolve our state through Bolshevism*); and then an economic word (= *they liquidate our money; swim in it; we have nothing*).

All you need is SS, said these bodies. Securitate, self-protection in echelons, a strictly hierarchic world: 'women' (and other forces that dissolve our bodies) in 'their place' (kitchens, beds, ghettos, graves).

But the object-choice of the 'comrade's sister' type also exists and existed elsewhere. It plays a large role wherever social access to the other sex is impeded.

Where else could one meet innocent girls (and the meeting had to be innocent in the 1950s, for instance) if not at one's friends' homes? And vice versa: where else could girls find harmless lads if not in the form of the brothers of their best friends or of their sisters' friends? The first sexual contacts of school pupils in the 50s and 60s were mostly with just such sisters or brothers, although the friend was no longer called a 'comrade' and the result of this love-choice was now rarely 'marriage'. But the constellation has lost none of its importance for these first contacts, especially in country districts where, as ever, a sister who goes to the disco with her brother (as a woman who is 'unbooked') is held in high regard by his friends if they are looking for women. The same applies to the 'unbooked' brother of the girl's best friend. (Transferable after marriage to 'love of my best friend's wife'/'love of my best friend's husband'.)

This love-choice depends very much on which men and women are actually within social reach and accessible. This triggers the affect.

The psychic constellation of this choice reveals an important deviation from Freud's construct of 'attachment': here the sexuality lies not on the parent–child level (and above all is not part of the 'mother–son' or 'father–daughter' genealogy), but rather on the child–child level. It is a form of object-choice which does not actually *avoid* the affinity to father or mother, but rather skirts around it.

Object-choice according to psycho-class
(position in the birth order).

The *affective* strength in relationships on the sibling level results from a similarity in the two people's respective positions in their birth orders. If men and women who form couples are asked where they come in the birth order, it often turns out that first-born children tend to be linked with others who are first-born, those from the middle with others from the middle, and the youngest with the youngest (or according to other distinctive correspondences in the birth order). Certain positions in the birth order seem to give rise to specific types of affect; an affect that recognizes and attracts similar forms in others. It is not difficult to see the reasons for this: if one assumes that parents always act out conflicts from their own childhood with their children, such as the conflict with one's own father with the first-born child, the relationship to one's mother with another child and so on (the highly differing demands that parents place on their various children stem from this), it becomes clear that the first-born children experience completely different sides of their parents than those who come last in the birth order. It would be no exaggeration to say that they grow up in a different psychic universe.

I am the 5th of 6 children and the youngest son, married to the youngest of three sisters. By and large my friends are and have been the younger or youngest members of a series: there is evidently a psychic odour which others scent in me and I in them, and which is reliable. People who regard me more or less automatically as a sort of 'grown-up' and talk with me accordingly generally have a similar position in their families. On the other hand, people who never stop addressing me as 'young man' on the bus or at the cash desk of the store are presumably among the first-born. The same with those who, hearing that I 'write books', first of all check (or adjust their noses accordingly) whether I know my alphabet (which, of course, I don't). But I can tell from reviews, for instance, just which sort of sibling affection is present in the writing.

It's my assumption that the transmission networks and fish-hooks of the sibling level play a more significant role in love-choices and marital forms for the majority of people *here* than the constellations in the Oedipal triangle, namely the mother–father–child level (that's my impression – it can't be proved). The New York psycho-historian Lloyd de Mause invented the term psycho-classes to denote such differences. Younger siblings belong to a different psycho-class from that of first-born children (just as children who have been beaten form a different psycho-class to those who have been cosseted). They have other patterns of perception and behaviour specific to that class, a different psychic chemistry. The special magnetism of attraction or repulsion that is also between them when forming a couple prompts one to speak of an object-choice according to the *dispositions of psycho-classes.**

----

*Psycho-classes on the telephone: those voices that are so insistent ('obtrusive') that it is impossible to get away, even though one wanted to put down the phone 10 times over. They belong to a psycho-class enemy; there's little danger of a honeymoon here.

In his later years, Freud, an *oldest son,* came up with a nice image of his own birth order when he said to Alexander, the youngest in the series, that the two of them were like the bookcover for the five sisters who were born in-between. Sigmund the front cover, Alexander the back. In-between 'the book' itself, in which was written the whole sexuality of the mystery of women, of the 'unconscious'. For myself, more an Alexander than a Sigmund, I have a distinct urge to add a few things to 'the front cover' of the Freud book that only the back cover knows (where the swallow sings of different things to a different tune*).

A question in passing: does love lean on others, or can it walk on its own?** Is the loved one here or perhaps there? Or is the other 'one's self'?

'Love' doesn't come off too well in the ways of falling in love that I have mentioned.

The affect which determines an object-choice of the attachment type is aimed at a person who is not present: a former, imaginary mother. This touches on an important question: is it easier to love bodies that are present or ones that are absent? Freud replies that it is the presence of an absent person which is loved in a current body.

Doesn't that mean that love affect is not conceded any particular power of its own, and the love-object is not conceded any particular existence of its own? That sexual satisfaction, the release of tensions, is oriented to earlier occurrences, and the present act of love is just a feeble imitation? A little sad, this sort of love.

I always found that the encounter with another body as an *alien* body, the mingling with some beautiful unknown, is the most beautiful feeling in the sexual embrace; contact with what one has

---

*The swallow that sings here and elsewhere in this and the first volume of the *Book of Kings* is from Friedrich Rückert's poem 'Aus der Jugendzeit': 'no swallow will return to you what you weep over, but the swallow sings, the swallow sings in the village as before' (Trans.).

**The German word *angelehnt* means both 'leaning on' and 'attached to', as in Freud's *Anlehnungstypus* or attachment type. (Trans.)

never experienced and *cannot experience* in any other way . . . not so much reunification (*CDU-love*), but rather a new kind of life.

> Throw off your blues and shoes and things
> and lay it down under the bed.
> Just wrap me up in your beautiful wings.

Doubtless there is no escaping the fact that love feelings are always for something that is present *as well as* something that is absent in the loved one. But must the absent part be connected with the past? Doesn't love affect possess all *three* aspects of time? If the thinker's ecstasies come from a *mixture of times,* why not the lover's?

Love affect cathects a person who *is here,* a person who *was here,* and seeks a third person who is to *become* manifest in the loved one. The third aspect of love, the *programming* side – certainly not the weakest aspect of the affect – tends to be neglected by Freud. The production of the desired figure in the love-object is often conducted with means which, with their curious mixture of unconscious fixity of purpose and conscious sense of expediency, are reminiscent of *strategies*; mating strategies, strategies for modelling the object. I shall describe a few shortly.

Generally the loved objects resist two of the three temporal perspectives from which the lover gazes at them: they do not wish to become what a mother or father once were, nor what the other's love wishes to make of them; they wish to be loved for what they *are.* This, the most frequently expressed wish of the loved ones, is the one least likely to be met by the lover. Evidently they do not rate the other's opinion of themselves, or not very highly. I have spent so long construing your ways and reproaching you, but in the end I wish nothing more than to have you and to have you just as you are, Freud wrote to his bride, Martha Bernays, at the end of a four-year engagement on 2 February 1886. In a few moments we shall see what came *before* this concluding wisdom (Freud's by no means unversed strategic attempts at remodelling his beloved into the person of his wishes).

When choosing according to the 'comrade's sister' model, one does not 'love' an object at all, but rather the avoidance of it.

Who or what and with what feelings does one love when marrying according to the third model: object-choice based on psycho-class, the position in the birth order? One marries a resemblance, a man or woman from the same situation. – Is this type of love one of those forms of what Freud calls narcissistic object-choice? For Freud, the narcissistic love-choice has four possible forms.

Here one loves

(a)   what one is oneself (one's own self),
(b)   what one was oneself,
(c)   what one would like to be,
(d)   the person who was a part of one's own self.

Forms (a) and (b) fit object-choice according to psycho-class. One loves in part 'what one is oneself' and 'what one was oneself', when, as an oldest son, one falls in love with an oldest daughter and vice versa. Form (c), loving 'what one would like to be', can also play a part (when a not quite perfect specimen of the 'oldest child' marries a perfect one). A sort of love for one's own psychic position.

It is possible that all of the forms of love-choice which Freud terms *narcissistic* belong genealogically to the child–child level (with the exception of form 'd', in which the mother is involved). Laplanche/ Pontalis have pointed to the overlap between this form and the attachment model. The mother was not 'known' in the same way one knew a sibling or knows oneself from one's place among one's siblings. The mother always also remains a fantastic figure from another world, from another power; the power of the father, like the power of having given life. The power of symbioses that engulf or make one happy. It might be concluded from this that in principle the affects from the child–parent genealogy are stronger than those originating on the child–child level. But when I look at the clinch in which some brother–sister pairs are locked, I doubt it. Presumably the *strength* of the affect is determined individually.

... so I had 2 make you mine.

*

Provisional findings: the object has enormous difficulties in assuming any real contours.

Perhaps it will assume some in the following, 'strategic' ways of falling in love, for which the Freudian concepts only fit to a limited extent.

Object-choice 'medial woman'. Object-choice according to the woman's technical advancement.

Artists work with *media* ... instruments ... materials ... pencils ... typewriters ... paints ... cameras ... computers ... projectors ... tape-recorders ... musical notation: they work within specific recording systems using specific recording techniques.

Very often they fall in love with women who have a special relationship to these recording methods. And often marry these women. In the *Book of Kings*, vol. 1, I described a number of such relationships. I will give a further example here, the marriage-choice of a person familiar or dear to most of you, the marriage of Alfred Hitchcock.

Alma Reville, who became Alma Hitchcock, was a cutter and writer of film scripts, the most important member of Hitchcock's team on his early films apart from the cameraman. Barely 5 foot tall and half his weight, at first she was more famous for her film work than Alfred. She was one of the few cutters to be mentioned in the film credits during the twenties, and featured in the plans of Michael Balcon, Hitchcock's first studio boss, as a woman about to take the leap forward and become a director herself. She continued to write occasional film scripts for other film-makers up till 1929, but from then on she worked solely for her husband. (Fewer ambitions, as the biographer says.)

Alma Reville is not just some woman in the film world, but rather was *the* woman most deeply associated with it in England at the time that Hitchcock started to make films, i.e. at the time that Hitchcock was establishing the economic base to become 'eligible for marriage' (career), as it is traditionally termed. Hitchcock waited until he was slightly above her in the studio hierarchy before proposing.

Oh my head is spinnin' ...

That was the traditional side of it. The modern aspect lies in a marriage to a woman who is as attached as can be to the technical medium in which the man works, and in a form of proposal which skilfully avoids the least thought that it might be the result of being in love:

The day I proposed to Alma she was lying in an upper bunk of a ship's cabin. The ship was floundering in a most desperate way and so was Alma, who was seasick. We were returning to London from Germany. Alma was my employee. I couldn't risk being flowery for fear that in her wretched state she would think I was discussing a movie script. As it was, she groaned, nodded her head and burped. It was one of my greatest scenes – a little weak on dialogue, perhaps, but beautifully staged and not overplayed.

– a description in which love appears as a dizzying feeling, but metamorphosed into a somewhat un-Freudian form.

> And suddenly I see you
> Did I tell you I need you
> Every single day of my life.

There have been numerous similar marriages or romances this century between directors and playwrights and actresses, dancers and other women performers, or between composers and singers, writers and typists or female psychoanalysts, film people and actresses, cutters, writers (Thea von Harbou*), painters and models, etc. *Medial women*: actresses/dancers/singers/models speak, perform, exhibit, sing, dance on stages, canvases and podiums the things that their inventive men have thought up for them. They are more or less media of their men on levels or in locations where the latter's bodies are unsuited. Or, as with the cutters, typists and psychoanalysts, they are involved directly and

---

*Thea von Harbou (1888–1954); author of, among others, the novel *Metropolis* which was filmed by her husband Fritz Lang. (Trans.)

. . . round and round and round and round.

technically with the recording medium in which the man works, are *media employees,* part of the apparatus that the men need in order to live (to produce).

Women psychoanalysts belong to this series by virtue of the new way they listen with their ears – *technical* recording (taken from the telephone and the gramophone) – which was, and is, extremely attractive not only to their patients, but also to male writers who record words (a special type of 'medial woman').

In 1938, Gottfried Benn* married one of three women with whom he made love, the one who was a typist, and, as emerges from his letters, primarily *because* she was a typist (to the outrage of the other two, who were both actresses).

Typist does not mean 'someone from the typing pool'. I shall not examine here how the typewriter, as a new means of recording the written word, altered the way writers wrote (as has the computer in recent years); suffice it to say that for Benn, for instance, who was banned in 1938 from publishing, a woman who could type was also something akin to the printed page that he lacked; the same applies to Brecht in exile, who liaised with the actress and typist Grete Steffin.

Not infrequently this sort of object-relationship ends with the death of the woman involved, as I have described in my book *Orpheus and Eurydice.*

In *this* context the tendency, which is also inherent in this form of marriage or love, to create sequences of partners should be noted. In a great many cases the artist-man changes the requisite medial woman when there are changes of direction, shifts of gear in his artistic production. If the man writes poems from the position of a Tristan who has forfeited his Isolde, he will take a Wagnerian singer as lover; if he is writing an opera libretto, he will start a relationship with a composer's wife – the names of the players are unimportant; anyone who examines the circles round

---

*Gottfried Benn (1886–1956): one of the most important of the Expressionist poets, who later consolidated his position as a major German writer after the Second World War. (Trans.)

his or her favourite artists will find much the same – the thunderbolt of love, which strikes unexpectedly, finds curiously uniform routes here; it's quite astonishing, enough to make one doubt that it comes from the blue.

'Fair enough, just like other people who marry their secretaries,' you'll say, 'or the top girl at college.' Everyday things one is accustomed to walk past without giving them a second thought, like a typewriter or an editing desk. Without doubt, very everyday forms of marriage: the secretary at her typewriter *is* the first of the medial women who uses this machine. The technically advanced woman in business precedes her colleagues in the sphere of artistic production. Tapping the keys as the signal for the start of a romance is as common as ever in both fields.

Are the Freudian forms of object-choice involved here? Well, not every cutter marries and even directors have mothers. Alma Reville was a dominant person (like Hitchcock's mother); she 'wore the trousers' in the marriage and could be linked in terms of her biography with Alfred's mother. However, there were several 1000 other women in England who could have filled this function; but only a couple who could fill the position of a wife who cut her husband's films and checked the quality of the film scripts – perhaps just this one person. That is a pretty turn-up, that the *sole possibility* for romantic love grew, if it was ever going to, in a film studio: revealed itself as child and master of a technique.

Is love sparked more and more often by the love partner's technical qualities/equipment? Present-day youth seems to answer 'yes' when it comes to their first loves: good transference devices and locations, clothes that transport, the appropriate space haircut and vehicles are just as much a part of love as the actual person who is loved. So do they choose, just like the 'old timers', *without any great love,* with the sole difference that they do of their own free will what others were compelled to do? Not at all. Teenage loves are somewhat different from object-choice. It's impossible to say whether the current simultaneity of physical contacts at dance classes and discos/fear of AIDS, the wish-to-be-single, to 'keep one's distance', and the furious grabbing at 'the object', of 'partner-choice based on shared interests' with the continuance of sexualities on the brother/sister model, whether this mixture, heated up with TV models' bodies and accompanying drugs, will make any decisive difference to the ways object-choice is made, or whether other, psychically, sexually, medially or economically determined love-choices will later carry the day: whether the *technical* will remain an extra ingredient.

However much certain aspects of attachment or the positions within the birth order are involved, in essence the technical object-choice offers the possibility of avoiding a maternal sexuality or the familial sister sexuality, namely biographical encodings and chasms, as were quite definitely present between a demanding mother, Emma Hitchcock, and a son, Al, twisting and squirming while inventing stories. Alma Reville-Hitchcock's skills are located several turns higher up the transformatory spiral of a life rotating round art and technology; Alfred's Emma-mother cannot reach that far. So one will find no 'explanations' on the level of an 'engulfing maternal sexuality' for the sort of chasms yawning in Hitchcock's films. More likely, one will find hints about its structure in the Alma–Alfred relationship.

It was a peculiar marriage and one that was remarkably long-lasting. Its duration may have resulted from the avoidance of a confusion, which has dogged and still dogs the majority of such relationships. As a rule the man in these constellations suffers from being unable to distinguish between wives and media employees, as if he did not know *who* and *what* he actually loves and *how* he should love it.

Hitchcock was clear in his mind in that he saw sexuality (after the obligatory birth of a single daughter, which crops with curious regularity in such relationships) as connected with his work, and not with his wife's body. His type of 'sport', he said, takes place above the belt, or more precisely above the collar. A common love of good food and of producing good films proved to be a lasting bond for the relationship; Alma Hitchcock showed up at the

shooting right until Alfred's last film. This was one of the longest
lasting and perhaps 'happiest' marriages this century (in public),
'bought' with the renunciation of the more customary types of
sexuality (or is that an old-fashioned English version of a way of life
which is in fact much more common?). At any rate: no confusion
of the spheres; Hitchcock knew what he 'loved' in Alma, and also
how to separate it from his obsession with certain blonde actresses
– likewise non-sexual in any of the customary ways. (An obsession
that Alma did not relish, but had to tolerate, says Donald Spoto,
Hitchcock's biographer, from whose book *The Life of Alfred Hitchcock: The Dark Side of Genius* this information has been taken.)

In the final analysis, this love-choice followed certain aims. It
thus seems sensible to ask how far it was based on conscious,
strategic decisions: are these merely disguised as love affect for the
period of courting? Hard to say. But the great fixity of purpose with
which 'the object' is selected in the object-choice *medial woman*
allows one to assume a large proportion of conscious actions.

At any rate the women's usefulness for certain of their husband's
productions does not remain unconscious. The sexuality of these
relationships is a *production sexuality*. There are forms of object-
choice where production sexuality determines whether love will
break out (and in all probability a *mixture* of mutually incompatible
forms of sexuality decide its end).

All you need is a particular balance between various sexualities:
production sexuality, the sexuality of physical contact, the sexuality
of obsessions with the 'beloved object in the distance', and so on.
The first is a highly intellectualized sexuality; in the second,
elements of love of the attachment type can be satisfied; in the
third, aspects of a 'narcissistic' choice: loving what one would like
to be in keeping with Freud's model c): e.g. tall, cool/seductive
blonde women when one is male, short, tubby, bald and not very
seductive (or seems to be).

Cleverer men, skilled in distinguishing between the different
types of sexuality, have attempted to satisfy their various needs
through relationships with differing types of women. This would

seem to be a socially viable method (it avoids deceptive scenarios, the embarrassing confusions between people and different ways of loving; it avoids *swapping* – exchanging one loved object for another with the *same* sort of sexuality – , which has and retains something humiliating and self-humiliating about it). Freud, as we shall see, was very good at making these distinctions.

It gets dangerous, though, when the phrase 'I really love you' appears in the sphere of production sexuality. The various orders of sensuality are divided by chasms (as Rilke saw); as are the various orders of love. Anyone who attempts to be present in two people with the one *body* that he/she has spans him/herself across abysses.* People play this game (some *only* play this one; its affect is called the *thrill of love* ... crashing to the ground is pre-planned).

Object. Choosing, being chosen. Subject.

Obviously those women who are loved according to the technical advancement model are not simply the 'object' of a choice; they're educated, often independent, self-confident, by no means the waiting daughter who is dependent on Someone arriving to rescue her from the Hades of the parental home. It is rare that the one who sets about choosing her is her first love; they have, have had and know men – what stirs them?

Two assumptions: presumably their choices are based more on the attachment model than those of the man involved, i.e. they are made less strategically; and, inasmuch as they choose and are chosen strategically on the basis of an anticipated use, they will share the man's strategies in pursuing his aims to a certain, if not a great, extent.

---

*The abyss between one home and the next, say: falling in love with the neighbour's wife, the neighbour's husband; a forced choice which both Moses and Luther attempted to forestall with one of their ten brief commandments. It arose from the limited choice of other love partners or locations, as well as from the inviting possiblity of bridging this abyss. Nowadays it is more a variety of keeping up with the Joneses. Possibly one's neighbour has the better model. Truffaut made a dreadful film about this, *The Woman Next Door* (deadly for all).

Just for a thrill you made my life a sad song.

The 'attachment' results from the fact that daughters who emancipate themselves, unmarried, from their parental homes and establish their independence have very often (as the intelligent daughters who have been given a lot of encouragement) had and maintained a special intellectual-affective relationship with their fathers. It is evident that they prefer to fall in love with the 'superior' intellectuality of creative men; in men who do not demand that they renounce their achievements; in men whose intellectuality resembles their own; in men who merely demand that they place their abilities in the service of the – 'superior' – cause of the man. There is a sense of election about the choice, and that presumably constitutes a large part of the bribe. Is it stupidity or a mistake to want to be *Brecht's* lover, enter relationships that advance one's own self and increase one's lust for life; relationships in which the woman does 1001 things that she *wants* to do; relationships which produce feelings of love which (at first) are without a sting? The love affects (a mixture of happy 'attachment' and the experience of widening horizons, the certainty of being loved and needed) are presumably stronger at the beginning of these relationships than in most other loves (substantiated *subject*-choice).

Perhaps these relationships would rarely break up (from the side of the women involved), or at least do so less often than they do: but the already mentioned tendency of the men in question to work through a sequence of women (strategic change of the love-object when changing the direction of one's production) provides the explosive force.

Second, perhaps what Freud termed the narcissistic tendency of productive women to prefer being loved than 'themselves to love' would mean that the man who casts a strategic eye on a suitable 'medial women' would be unable to tie her to his production simply as a media employee; 'love' must be involved if he is to win her for the task (and thus he creates – and confuses – both: media employee *and* lover). But it is also possible that this is a characteristic of the self-affirming male thirst for conquest, to which the 'object' is unable to add little or nothing. Women will know more about this.

Little Miss Strange ...

Object-choice in an institution (1). Alma mater.

In 1924, while studying philosophy at Marburg University, the 18-year-old Hannah Arendt fell in love with the philosophy professor Martin Heidegger, and he, about twice her age, in her. In the words of Hannah Arendt's biographer, Elisabeth Young-Bruehl, Heidegger *'admitted'* to his lover some twenty years later that she had been the inspiration for his work in those years, the impetus to his passionate thinking.

The product of this passionate thinking was *Being and Time*, Heidegger's main philosophical work. The affair was kept as secret as possible; Heidegger was married, his wife Elfride and their two children lived in the town – but complete secrecy between professor and student is impossible. The rays spreading from an intellectual love cannot be hidden from those who want or have to see them. When she noticed her husband's affection, Elfride Heidegger treated the young Jew from Königsberg 'coolly'.

It is the nature of things (i.e. of the university profession) that professors & female doctorands fall in love, and especially susceptible are radiant freshers (who in turn make others weak): so bright, so different, so young, so sexual, so Jewish – merry and melancholy at the same time – this woman, half his age and so knowledgeable ... he wasn't used to that, was entranced, as was she. What female student, 18 and willing to listen, open to the spirit and tone of the lecture rooms and male character and male tongues, would want to resist? Nor did she want to resist, she wanted to love what she heard, and did so.

By 1925 Elfride Heidegger was already openly anti-semitic and openly Nazi. She invited her husband's students (reports Günther Stern, who later named himself Günther Anders, the author of those beautiful books on *Die Antiquiertheit des Menschen* [The Antiquatedness of Man]), to join the National Socialist student group in Marburg. She also invited Stern, then 'turned her back' on him when he replied he was different, a Jew. A few years later Günther Stern was to become Hannah Arendt's first husband.

... *came out of the darkness.*

Being and Time gained by transgressing to the beyond, to the Hades of a Jewish-philosophical lover (and as far beyond his own wife as imaginable) – even works are brought to the world by couples. Permitted: the works; desired. Forbidden: the couples, or passed over in silence. Here more than elsewhere 'the parents get divorced'.

Heidegger did not wish to change anything, or see anything changed in his life as a result of this brilliant young Jewess's ardent love (as Arendt's biographer writes), and furthermore the moment came in the summer of 1925 when Hannah Arendt realized that he was to remain a stranger, no matter how deeply tied they were.

Heidegger passed Arendt on to his friend in Heidelberg, Karl Jaspers, to complete her doctorate which she could hardly work on any more under him. She gained her doctorate under Jaspers (who was married to a Jew and remained so; he and Heidegger were soon to fall out) with a thesis on Augustine's concept of love.

She realized later that her love for Heidegger in Marburg was a devotion to a single one and set about discovering other poles.* 'Devotion to a single one' is never without its dangers; especially when that 'single one' is a man on the academic ladder.

Jaspers finally discovered that Heidegger's philosophy *lacks love*, and Hannah Arendt deemed that the basic character of this self is its being-for-itself, its radical detachment from its peers.

– so what did they see in him? The beams of light radiating from the thinker – without love? Is the philosophical mind so easily deceived? Or is it a case of institutional coercion in the state organizations of the male-philosophical spirit (state inside the state) within male couples and, once the portals had been opened for participating women, likewise within heterosexual couples?

Later, as power entered Heidegger and he loved her once more, Hannah Arendt remained 'loyal' to him (as far as an emigrant Jew could to a member of the NSDAP; she said nothing).

---

*In vol. 1 of the *Book of Kings*, the author contrasts a notion of multipolarity with the adhesion to a restricted number of bipolar dimensions that led Gottfried Benn (among millions of others) to court Fascism in the thirties. (Trans.)

It would not be wrong to see Heidegger's part in expelling the Jews from the university as also a small attempt at making up with his wife. At last a glimmer of pardon in Elfride Heidegger's eyes –

Martin at the head of the university squad, boots (stacked-up heels), SA jacket, guards of honour with swastikas, waving flags (purgatorio) ... academic comedies played by country lads who were thus brought to the derelict throne of philosophy.

Even after the war was 'won' (how could it have been 'won'?) no act of revenge from Hannah Arendt, now herself a professor in the USA. For the sake of her former great love she chose to assume that he had never denounced anyone.

She acted according to the tenet of her other teacher, Karl Jaspers, that one never says '*no*' to someone to whom one has already said '*yes*'. That's also very nice and necessary for preserving one's own nice self.

She wrote to Karl Jaspers, though, saying she wished that the whole generation, her generation, were already dead.

Did her decision not to attack Heidegger in public, even after the war, derive from the type of love-choice that had united them in the twenties? Presumably, for this union was based on a certain reciprocity: during her relationship with the professor, the young student first becomes a doctorand and then a philosopher in her own right. Her love-choice was directed at 'what she herself wanted to become' (Freud's narcissistic type of love-choice (c)) – and it worked.

Heidegger's amorous transgression with the Jewish student was also directed at something which he wished to become or rather produce: a work whose foundations she became a part of (and not as a dead body).

There was also a form of reciprocity in their transgression, directed at an existing marriage: the Jew Hannah Arendt was aware of the anti-semitism of Heidegger's wife; her intellectual superiority over his wife and her political superiority was in many ways a sweet connecting link in their liaison, allowing them to feel 'in the right', for the two of them belonged together much more than Heidegger and his Elfride – the story almost shouts it out loud. And then there would also not have been a Nazi Heidegger.

... and stood beneath the lights.

That is probably a fallacy, for this sort of love match does not bear the mark of the royal children;* much clearer is the inherent tendency to create sequences of partners.

Doctorands come and go, that's in the nature of universities; and as long as this remains patriarchal, the doctoral supervisor** is not simply father or man, but rather chief baboon in the scientific horde. It is also part of the construction of the institution that he appears as a sexual authority and the emerging academic-women as sexual objects for the academic-primates; even if it is not an actual dictate, this form of love is at least a commandment of the institution, just as the love relationship between boss and secretary is a commandment ('seduction') of a different kind of institution – the 'office' in the so-called 'free market'. The commandment very often leads to marriage, but even more frequently to something else, to sequences. It is not the wives who are swapped (in both cases), but rather the secretaries. And likewise female doctorands come and go.† (Like the sixth-form girls in whom the teachers are not allowed to fall in love, but *must*.)

It is a feature of some institutions that they *dictate* specific ways of making object-choices, while penalizing the accompanying amorous contacts. The school is one of them (I shall not say anything about churches here).

Lightning strikes. Blitzkrieg strategies.
Object-choice as symptom.

The 48-year-old writer Knut Hamsun fell in love with the actress Marie Andersen *on the spot.* She tried to do the same. She was

---

*The royal children is an image from a German folk ballad based on the legend of Hero and Leander: two royal children fall in love, but are separated by a deep river (the deep waters that keep running through the present work). The prince swims the waters every night by the light of a candle so that they may be united, but one night the candle is extinguished by a nun wishing them ill and he drowns. (Trans.)

**Doktorvater* in German, which means literally 'doctorate father'. (Trans.)

†A study of suicide among female doctorands would be valuable in this connection, commented women who attended my lectures.

supposed to act in a play by Hamsun. Hamsun happened to be in Oslo at the time. The theatre director seized the opportunity and arranged a meeting in the theatre café.

Hamsun descended on HER, exclaiming 'how beautiful' she was . . . admired her hands . . . they *compared* their hands ('that will bring bad luck,' she said) . . . 'Angel's hands,' he said . . . and 'how old are you?' . . .

The next day, 26 half-open roses. Had he spent the whole night reading Storm?*

> The nightingale, it can, it does
> Sing the whole night long
> Sweetly regaled, bursts forth the rose
> To its darling song.

Hamsun hated actors (actresses). Love at first sight with a member of a 'hostile race' at the age of 48? That so common love of one's 'opposite'? . . . the constantly suppressed hitting back as spontaneous object-choice?

'Object-choice' indeed: she was showered with letters, instructions . . . drops of blood . . . admissions of his madness. Why 'YOU'?

At the first moment of their meeting – this can be said quite clearly – Hamsun decided that this was the woman for whom he was searching (for particular ends). At that very first moment he discovered that this woman, who was a well-known artist on the verge of becoming 'the leading actress' of the Norwegian National Theatre in Oslo, also harboured two other women: on the one hand, the unhappy first love of his youth, with whom he still had an account to settle; on the other, the features of a country woman, which allowed him to revive a side of his departed mother, with whom he also had an account to settle. Third, she was active in the competing medium 'drama', while he was on the way to establishing prose, the novel, as the leading art form in Norway; a lover

---

*Theodor Storm (1817–1888): German poet and writer who bridged Romanticism and Realism. (Trans.)

whose body helps one perform such a turnabout is not the worst proof of one's own qualities as a lover or writer.

Or was it enough for Hamsun to have discovered in this grown-up Marie's infatuated eyes the gaze of the schoolgirl who had been in love with Hamsun's writing . . . a *reader* . . . bound to him (behind her desk at school) for ever and a day . . . ?

What creates the thunderbolt (which is transformed so rapidly into a blitzkrieg)?

Hamsun achieved three things in a short space of time: he utterly destroyed the actress in his wife; second, he made a countrywoman of her; third, he removed her from the city of Oslo to the rural seclusion close to the polar circle, the very location of his first adolescent love. There are patterns in Marie Andersen's lifelines that are identical to the life of his adolescent love. Hamsun *could* not know that at the moment *he set eyes on her.* But he had seen it.

This constellation allows him to write a novel for which he receives the Nobel Prize, during the writing of which he distances himself completely from his wife and their children (he views the births as bothersome competition). Award of the Stockholm Prize and irreparable ruin of the marriage coincide. This door was destined just for you, says the door-keeper. . . . You were just for this novel, says the keeper of the found treasure. . . . Marie Andersen's strategic use was over.

The prospect of making Hamsun the 'king of poets' (as she put it in one of her letters) had been enough to make her accept his proposal (one can say: likewise at the first moment). She felt she could manage it, and she was right. He really did become the king for all (as he already was for the girl behind her school desk), but she became just a step to this throne, and not his queen. 'At first sight –'

**Can you see me baby?
I don't believe you can.**

Ill-matched couples.
Object-choice of the certain-to-find-the-wrong-partner type.

Many ways of loving must be brought into play before the
construction of the 'thunderbolt' can be described: attachment
model, choice according to psycho-class, narcissistic modes of
choice (a), (b) and (c), choice based on the medial position of the
woman ... they all contribute to the intensity with which the *moment*
ignites ... but a closer look at the course of these loves leads to the
conclusion that the person chosen this way was destined above all
to be used, sometimes to be *used up* ... one of those well-prepared
experiments with a fatal outcome.
　... there's a spark ... something catches ... clicks ... snaps into
place ... two people get together ... ('why *them* of all people?', say
their friends ... they're the last people who should become 'one')
... they're not at all *suited*. Everyone sees that the 'couple' which is
in the process of creating itself, as if it was the first of its kind, is
built of anything but *love*. (Everyone apart from the couple itself.)

　'There are *nothing* but wrong couples' I hear a friend of mine say.
(And I feel relieved to see the pair of which I am one half as one
of the impossible exceptions.)

　Why do the 'wrong people' keep liaising? Is *object-choice* itself the
mistake? A form of deception, self-deception? What's the point of
thunderbolts when it's clear to others (and soon enough those
involved) that it's all about ends? And soon enough purely about
survival. Is it true what the cynics among the artists say, that 'the
women' won't do what 'the man' wants if love is not included in the
bouquet? Yesterday evening good old Philippe Noiret repeated it
on TV in a Chabrol film.
　Does the male strategic courtship which succeeds in looking like
ardent affect summon up an affect among women who are
genuinely able to satisfy the diverse strategic wishes of the man, an
affect that rises from a desire for self-destruction and self-punishment?
　The readiness for self-destruction and self-punishment derives

from earlier experiences which have been stored in the body, but not in consciousness or 'memory'; traumas that demand to be acted out; which are unable to tell their tales except in ever-repeated actions; unconscious guilt feelings are *the store*, in the body, for what others have done to it.

Must a strategy collide with a guilt so that a thunderbolt leaps out and illuminates, in the few seconds as it strikes, the field of something 'forbidden' from the past in which the outlines of future outrages appear just as briefly, before those involved sink, thunderstruck, into one another's arms and abandon themselves to their fate (i.e. to a plan and a self-destructive 'desire')?

SHE seems capable of meeting this man's special demands; perhaps of being the *sole person* who can do so. A strong surge of narcissistic affect: 'I *am* the princess who can make a king of this man,' must be involved; the road to self-injury veiled by a strongly narcissistic gain from illness. The choice itself: a symptom of this illness.

On the other hand, *intentions*: someone wants to bring a story to light that he/she does not *know* him/herself; which is well known as fertile soil for Freudianized policemen. It is described coolly in a sentence I found in an American crime novel: It wasn't the first ill-matched couple I'd ever met, as V.I. Warshawski, woman private detective in Sara Paretsky's *Burn Marks*, says to herself, faced by a couple (this time two wrongly-matched men), the one half of which wanted to give her a rough time; but, odd as things are, it will prove to be a life-saving act.

Perhaps it is not even a rare feature of object-choice of the certain-to-find-the-wrong-partner type. Whoever carries the burden of dark episodes will be unable to resolve them in easy loves. *Love* here is anything but *all you need*; what's needed is a doctor, a story and history doctor.

Why do *ill-matched couples* stick so firmly together? Because the 'wrong partner' is just the right one for reviving the unfinished body history, getting to grips with repetitions, for settling old accounts, in the lightning bolt of a blackout.

Woman, oh woman, don't treat me so mean

*

In 'The Taboo of Virginity', Freud (starting from Hebbel's *Judith**) makes the observation that some women are unable to separate themselves from men they do not love because they have not *completed* their revenge (in this case revenge for the violation of the woman's virginity).

Some *women*? Incapable of proper object-love, are they nevertheless capable of full acts of revenge (beheading; castration) out of injured love? Freud's idea would have been more dazzling if he had applied it to both sexes and removed it from the idea of virginity. Diving into unresolved histories through clinches, obsessions and the quasi-murderous use of the love-object is certainly *not* a female privilege.

The couples play on the edge of the precipice, waiting to see whether the lightning bolt or the dark engulfment of the lover will reveal the doctor, or the cop, the killer or someone else. In Hitchcock's *Vertigo* it's the cop who appears in the lover. It's more thrilling that way. In life, which is more boring, the thunderbolt might also give birth to figures who are not called Dr Strangelove.

Object-choice 'The bird in the bush' (is better than 10 in the hand).
Social climbing marriages, love for the boss's daughter, colonial
strategies.

Men on their way up like to fall in love with the daughters of men with higher positions in society. And there's a risk of *object-choice* and marriage when the daughter belongs to a man occupying the social position the *upward climbing man* wishes to reach. Social ascent is documented by the acquisition of a wife from the social stratum one has reached or wishes to reach. Object-choice according to the model: marrying the daughter of the boss, the political

---

*Friedrich Hebbel (1813–1863), one of the most important German playwrights of the nineteenth century, introduced a new form of realism with his first play *Judith* (1840), a tragedy based on the Old Testament story of Judith who killed the commander Holofernes. (Trans.)

leader, the backer, the boss, the leader of the pack.

The French medical student (and later writer) Louis-Ferdinand Céline (poor) marries the daughter of a doctor (not so poor), who is head of a private hospital. Through this marriage he advances (deputizing for the chief doctor) to become the designated successor to the professor/head of the hospital. With this goal before him, exams completed, the bird in the hand (and now father of a daughter), he notes that he wants to be and become something else than chief doctor and leaves his wife.

Later, when he has dedicated his life first and foremost to the dissolution of French grammar ... to the dance of words ... and at the same time particularly enjoys watching ballet dancers glide along (which captures the aim of his writing so beautifully), he marries a dancer. (The marriage lasts till death did them part ... Lucette Destouches administers his estate to this day.)

In between times there were a number of proposals, *attempted* marriages with Jewish women which are *also* linked with the fact that, in the twenties, Céline considered a particular stratum of intelligent and well-off Jews alone capable of bringing political order to the world, and a few Jewish women (expelled from Germany) alone capable of doing the same with his mind. I am most grateful to you for introducing me to Annie Reich. She is every bit as nice as my other girl friends from Central Europe, and that's saying something. She has told me thousands of incredibly useful things and has made me almost intelligent within the space of a few days. (Céline in July 1933 to Cillie Pam. Annie Reich and Wilhelm Reich are just in the process of separating. One of his 'other girl friends' is Annie Angel, psychoanalyst and member of the Socialist Association for Sexual Counselling and Social Research in Berlin.) Céline's attempts to *become a Jew,* to put it pointedly, failed. He became an *ardent* anti-semite (for this and other reasons). (Just as a number of men who in recent years made long, futile efforts *to become women* are no longer exactly card-carrying members of the Friends of Feminism.)

Love follows a strange logic along strange paths. Love is sparked by women who are like a guarantee of the social positions which the man wishes to reach, by class membership, racial background, production possibilities. The biographies of politicians are full of marriages between young male climbers and the daughters of influential party leaders (and love affairs with women in the limelight; three dancers/singers/actresses in Winston Churchill's life, for instance). Love is kindled by women who are situated at the reference points of one's own life plan. The film-maker François Truffaut marries a producer's daughter. On the cover of *Bringing It All Back Home*, Bob Dylan is sitting by the fireplace (= home) with Sally Grossman, the wife of his manager; he married her friend Sarah Lowndes.

Variations: the sons of workers who when setting out on university or state careers marry the daughters of civil servants; the sons of junior civil servants who fall in love with the daughters of businessmen or lawyers while emancipating themselves from the status of state property to become self-employed. Apprentices who rise to become social workers via polytechnics who liaise with committed female students. Upward mobility in craftsman's workshops, small industrial firms ... here it's the boss's daughter. Colonial: the compulsory love for the wife or daughter of the *white master.*

On the other hand, male colonialists like to marry the daughter or sister of the native chieftain. Not just in South Seas novels or the love for Winnetou's* sister, not just in Joseph Conrad's *Lord Jim*, not just as male fantasy: these marriages have always been a concrete part of colonial politics. From Cortés onwards, the native chieftains' daughters have been tied to the white conquerors by marriage or marriage-like relationships. Cortés marries Montezuma's daughter. Doña Marina, the daughter of another chieftain, is his lover and interpreter. In North America it is the chieftain's daughter Pocahontas who, through her relationship with the commander of the whites, John Smith, and her later marriage with the planter John Rolfe, assures the survival of the whites on numerous occasions. She learns the language, then the

---

*Winnetou is the Red Indian hero of a series of adventure stories written by the German author Karl May (1842–1912). (Trans.)

. . . I don't know, she wouldn't say.

religion of the conqueror, who thus appears to cease being a conqueror, but who can only now erect his work undisturbed (i.e. without losing his life) on a firm foundation (in which later this woman lies, dead).

As soon as the new stratum, the 'new country' have actually been reached, the climber/conqueror makes a curious yet quite self-evident discovery: there are a number of these 'sole persons', perhaps even many, who at a stroke are potentially within arm's reach. This 'sole person' whom he has married promptly breaks down under the weight of this observation. One could term this an *object-disintegration*, occurring when strategic goals have been reached (once again the step that lays the foundation stone for *forming possible sequences of partners* is easily seen).

Separation from these daughters is often impossible because of the coalition involved. They are retained as representatives of status attained and of a social-paternal power (and perhaps even highly regarded in this role), but the husband's affects depart and turn to other forms of object-choice.

What does Narcissus love when he loves himself?

Modified slightly, the narcissistic form of choice (c), loving what one would like to be oneself, can be used to describe object-choice according to the social climbing strategy model: loving or marrying the object which helps one become what one wishes to be or wishes to be in future.

It could be said that this is more a form of love of oneself than for the chosen object. But this does not allow for any description of the tactical-strategic-male-state characteristics that reveal themselves in this type of choice. If both aspects are considered, the picture of a *highly versed strategic narcissism* emerges – a seductive mixture of intentions and affects.

What sort of mixture of feelings does the man in question have? I don't believe that he plays at 'being in love'. Nor do I believe that the daughters concerned would let themselves be deceived by this.

39

You need some guiding, baby ...

It must be a very special mixture of affects, one that is triggered at the moment a particular female object enters the man's strategic plans as a 'suitable lover' (as an incredibly suitable lover): the curious ability to enter (in one's own eyes and in those of the woman who is being courted) an 'extreme state of infatuation' which actually manages to appear to be 'love'.

The objects of this form of choice reveal an astonishingly diminished ability to resist. It could even be said that they show an extraordinary readiness to take part in this form of wooing, which is performed with the whole gamut of flattering attentions, exaggerations and tricks.

What does the man *love about himself* that turns him into him the successful, desiring man? The answer is simply: he loves himself for his ability to achieve the target on which he has set his sights. Self-love ('self-certainty') radiates from him like a form of power and makes him 'attractive'. The love of the capacity to love one's own methods is so great that it unhesitatingly incorporates the people it needs to reach the beloved goal. The 'love' of the women involved would be a sort of union with the radiant strategist's power of self-love (just as now the GDR ostensibly, or really, loves Mr Kohl).

This sort of love is dependent on an enormous (socially endorsed) male self-overvaluation and the social and personal weaknesses of women. Neither seem to be particularly on the wane at present.

The unalloyed love that any old male dipshit has for himself is one of the current capital crimes in the face of history.

The *love* object continues to be hard to discern.

When nowadays women talk about how they are fed up with being idealized and then being used for some end, they stress that women are not *better* than men but simply *different*. Perhaps not better, but certainly only half as nasty (at least when it comes to self-irradiating love, the male form of being good mates with the world).

* * *

. . . I'm just deciding, baby.

I look at you all
See the love there that's sleeping
While my guitar gently weeps.

II. Fragment of a Freud biography

Freud's choice

In the beginning was – ? A sweet girl: Martha is mine, the sweet girl, of whom everyone speaks to me with great admiration, who captivated me from our first meeting, however much I resisted –

– the 'first meeting' was two months earlier. It is June 1882, Martha Bernays and Sigmund Freud are newly engaged, but separated; the post travels back and forth between Vienna and Wandsbek near Hamburg. This is the fiancé's first letter, 19 June 1882, to be followed by fifteen hundred others until the process of 'object-choice' is concluded in 1886.

In the beginning was – a resistance? A resistance, a bolt of lightning, captivation.

A chance acquaintanceship with Freud's 5 sisters led the bride to the groom's house, where Sigmund and Martha met for the first time, notes Ernst Freud, the 4th child and youngest son, born 10 years after the event, in his introduction to the edition of Freud's letters.

Object-*finding*, in accordance with the 'sister's friend' model, is involved, then the 'lightning flash', which, two months later, has turned into ownership: Martha is mine, the sweet girl –

And more. Freud's sentence from his first *letter to his bride* continues (still referring to the 'sweet girl') as follows: whom I was afraid to court, and who, responding with generous trust, raised my belief in my intrinsic worth and gave me new hope and energy to work, just as I desperately needed them.

– 'whom I was afraid to court' and the raising of his belief in his intrinsic worth allow the conclusion that a bride from a higher (social) stratum is being wooed; the first present that she has brought to this liaison is the increase in her loved one's work energy (something he desperately needed, as he says).

The forms found in social climbing marriages ... object-choice as a symptom ('bolt of lightning') . . . choice of a sister's friend . . . choice based on the bride's usefulness for the man's energies . . . are all involved; that casts a curious light on a word in Ernst Freud's description, the little word *chance* before the word acquaintance-ship.

In a case like this, chance is probably not the mother of attachment.

A young scientist in Vienna, neurologist, assistant at the Physio-logical Institute, 26 years old, very talented, on his way to a professorship or a private practice, coming from a poor (and somewhat dishonest) eastern Jewish trading family, wavering between Jewish orthodoxy and assimilation into the Western-natural-scientific (= atheist) university world, is thinking of mar-riage around 1880 – what should his model-wife look like? She would have to be daughter of a doctor or some other professor, from a Jewish, Western-assimilated family, and the family wealthier than his own. Right?

Freud's choice is not very far removed. **Martha Bernays, writes Ernst Freud, came from a not unimportant family from Wandbek near Hamburg. Her grandfather Isaac (Chacham) Bernays was an eminent rabbi in the city of Hamburg. Her two paternal uncles are important figures in German cultural history.**

He is speaking here of two professors. One, Michael Bernays, was an important Goethe and Shakespeare scholar, the first ever professor of modern German literary history (at Munich Uni-versity) and for a while reader to Ludwig II of Bavaria. The other, Jacob Bernays, professor of classical philology at Bonn University, was the first non-baptized Jewish professor at a German university. Martha's father was no longer alive when she met Freud; he was not a professor but a merchant, like Freud's father, if better placed, more assimilated to the West and not quite so dubious: Berman Bernays, in his last years, was assistant to the Viennese economist Lorenz von Stein. One of the uncles was also dead, Professor Jacob Bernays. He died one year before the engagement. The other uncle, Michael Bernays (the only one of the three brothers to abandon the Jewish faith, and who is, moreover, a Wagnerian), is alive and acts as the couple's father-in-law, together with Martha's brother Eli, who has supported the family after the father's death (and soon marries Freud's sister Anna). So even if Freud doesn't fall in love with a daughter-from-the-hand-of-a-professor, then at least he does so with a niece encoded with two professor uncles ... daughter from the realm which he himself wishes to enter, and a daughter from that type of family in which he wishes to climb/be converted, away from the Galician-orthodox tradesman's world of his own.

All that could still be a result of Ernst Freud's 'chance' or the theory of probabilities. The importance of this constellation for Freud's love affect would be quite undemonstrable were it not for Freud's own game with it; and this contains a number of surprises of a very special kind.

The reason for this is that the uncles were very special professors. One was a Goethe and Shakespeare specialist; the other a classical philologist and specialist in Aristotle – neither of them professors of medicine, but it was Freud's intention to become not a simple professor of medicine, but, rather, something which both these uncles stand for.

Uncle Jacob Bernays had devoted particular attention to Aristotle's concept of catharsis, and published on it between 1852 and 1880. Freud's biographer Sulloway remarks:

In Vienna, as elsewhere, this whole subject was much discussed among scholars and in the salons and even assumed for a time the proportions of a craze. According to Hirschmüller, by 1880 Bernays's ideas had inspired some seventy German-language publications on catharsis, a number that more than doubled by 1890.

Naturally this will ring a bell among readers of Freud's early works: '*cathartic method*' is the first term Freud gave to what he later called the psychoanalytic method. The term came from his essay 'On Hysteria' (1895), and was elucidated in his description of the treatment of Anna O., who herself referred to it loosely as *chimney sweeping*. Sulloway concludes, it seems very possible that an intelligent girl like Anna O. might have been acquainted with the subject and unconsciously have incorporated this knowledge into the dramatic plot of her illness – the only objection to which might be that there is a somewhat ineradicable tendency among psychoanalytic authors to attribute the knowledge and procedures of 'intelligent' girls to the unconscious. If in the case of the intelligent Anna O. – i.e. Bertha Pappenheim, a friend of Martha's – the *cathartic method* came, as Sulloway suggests, directly (even if unconsciously) from Martha's uncle Jacob, then it has to be said in favour of Freud, who not did not merely know his uncle's works unconsciously, that, together with Breuer, he chose to refer his 1895 publication to, among others, this uncle and to present himself to the public within this particular genealogy as the heir to the catharsis specialist Jacob Bernays and as the husband of his niece Martha.*

After 1895, Freud's collaboration with Breuer comes to an end, as do his hope of emancipating the *talking cure, catharsis,* and turning it into *psychoanalysis.* (Instead of which, Freud discovered the sexual abuse of daughters as the cause of hysteria; a truth which is, however, a hindrance to the development of psychoanalysis.)

When in 1897 he begins to elevate the interpretation of dreams to the 'royal road to the unconscious' and shift it to the centre of the psychoanalytic method, he shows his debt to Martha's other uncle, the Goethe/Shakespeare Bernays, by littering the description of his breakthrough to *dream interpretation* with quotes from Goethe and Shakespeare. In Freud's writing of October 1897, Hamlet and Oedipus are still contesting the principal role in the psychoanalytic scenario. And Freud describes the importance of

---

In addition to this comes Freud's own involvement with Aristotle. Freud wrote a text entitled 'On the Means/Media which Poets Are Accustomed to Use in Matters of Love' that drew on Aristotle and was published eight years before his engagement to Martha when he was studying under the Aristotle specialist Franz Brentano in Vienna. ('De mediis, quibus in amoribius efficendis utuntur poetae.'*) The Aristotelian influence Freud received from Bretano made him waver seriously in 1874 between doing his doctorate in medicine or in philosophy. The double doctorate (which he had always wished for) was given a new lease of life by his bride, who was linked with Aristotle, but who was only first initiated into this and more in Freud's letters during the following years.

dreams – as the store room of one's personal history – with three lines from a poem by Goethe.*

The references to the works of Professors Jacob and Michael Bernays are a notable component of Freud's publications and writings up to 1899. Chance? Game? Bows to Martha? Proof that he really does belong in the 'new family'? How better to emphasize this than by linking one's own work with that of the famous uncles. Freud, like all founding heroes, is busy providing himself with a new history; creating his own self anew, but in a way different to that adopted by his own parents. The woman who is chosen for marriage is *always* of special importance for this revision of the husband's origins and history; she leads him to other historical worlds; is intended to lead him to them. Martha seems well suited to play a special part in this. Freud told her the part she was to be assigned just four weeks after their engagement; a *programme* for Martha.

Hamburg, July 1882. While looking for a printer for writing paper which was to bear a personal monogram, Freud stumbles across the tracks of another Bernays, Martha's grandfather Isaac; a gift of providence (or result of shrewd researches) which Freud, in a letter to Martha dated 23 July 1882, uses to masterful effect. It is a letter and yet it is not a letter. As is later often the case when Freud chooses to elaborate one of his case-novellas, the letter adopts a literary pose. He does not address it to *My dearest* or *Martha*, as otherwise in his letters; it lacks both an opening address and a signature, but talks of Martha, a character in a tale, in the third person. Martha, literized, reads the following:

My girl came from a scholarly family and wrote – at first just letters – with an untiring hand, spending her small amount of money on stationery. Consequently I needed paper for this sweet, industrious child to write on, and chose some which she could use only to write to me.

---

*See the letters to Wilhelm Fließ of September and October 1897.

An intimately entwined M and S, such as only the magnanimity of the engravers could grant, made the sheets of paper unusable for any other purpose than the correspondence between little Martha and me. The man from whom I ordered this despotic paper one Friday did not want to deliver it before Sunday, because we're not here Saturdays, he said. It's an old custom of our's. Oh, how well I know these old customs. . . .

– like her learned uncles, Martha is to develop from letter writing to literary work, and this M & S headed note paper is for practice (just as he himself is once again practising at being a writer in this letter); after this first part of his hopes for the programme, the text moves on to the figure of the old engraver who feeds Freud with Jewish adages, which Freud translates into more germane words of wisdom, interlaced with phrases from love letters: Jerusalem has been destroyed and little Martha and I are alive and happy . . . which are then turned into philosophy of history: if Jerusalem had not been destroyed, the Jews would have been wiped out like so many peoples before and after us. Only with the collapse of the visible temple did the invisible construction of Judaism become possible. After this convoluted introduction comes the heart of the story, the 'unheard of event'; the old man's narration:

We owe our education to *one* man. In earlier years Hamburg and Altona formed a single Jewish community; which later divided; teaching was performed by subordinate teachers until the introduction of the reform in Germany. People then acknowledged that something had to be done, and called upon a certain Bernays who was made a 'Chacham'. This man educated us all. He wanted to tell me about all that he had accomplished, but I was more interested in the man himself. Did he come from Hamburg? No, he came from Würzburg, where Napoleon I had permitted him to study. (O how the peoples spin their legends!) [O how Freud spins his legend while reconstructing his history!] He came here as a very young man, and still lived here thirty years ago. Did you know his family? 'I grew up with his sons you know.' I now mentioned two names, Michael Bernays in Munich, and Jacob Bernays in Bonn. That's them, he confirmed, and there was also a third son who lived and died in Vienna. I also knew something about this third son, whose name remained in the shadow of the other brothers. [Berman Bernays, Martha's father whose name Freud likewise doesn't mention in his story.] The father's bountiful nature was shared among the sons. The father was a philologist, exegetist, and left important children behind him. One of the children stayed with language, which provided him with enough material to occupy him for the length of his academic career, the other still teaches respect for the fine taste and wisdom shown in the writings of our great poets and teachers. The third, an earnest, withdrawn man, had an even deeper comprehension of life than that provided by either art or science; he was simply a model of humanity and created new treasures [= daughters] instead of interpreting the old ones. All honour to the remembrance that little Martha has given me of him.

If only this old Jew, who now began to speak enthusiastically of his master's teachings, had suspected that his customer, ostensibly one Dr Wahle from Prague, had that morning kissed the grand-daughter of this man he admired so much. He related more memories from his youth, and now assumed something of the character of Nathan the Wise.

This is something like a whim (whim on a knife edge), presenting himself to the old engraver (and the reader of the letter) as 'Dr Wahle': friend of Freud and a former admirer of Martha, Ernst Freud mentions in a note. A game with identities and with the figure of the victor in courting the bride; and not only does Napoleon have to be included in the genealogy, but also Nathan the Wise and Lessing,* whose monument in Gänsemarkt in Hamburg is alluded to at the beginning of the letter, continuing an

---

*Gottfried Lessing (1729–1781): German playwright whose liberal humanitarianism was given foremost expression in his play *Nathan the Wise*. The 'ring parable' that Nathan relates in act three is one of religious tolerance and understanding: a man from the East possessed a ring that empowered its owner to appear pleasing to God and man alike. Aware that death is approaching, he allows two copies to be made of the ring, so that each of his three sons may inherit one. The three rings prove to be so alike that no one can say which is the *real* one, just as no one can say which religion (Christianity, Judaism or Islam) is the true one. (Trans.)

old game with Lessing. On the day of their engagement, 17 June 1882, Martha had presented him with her father's ring. Freud, who wore the ring on his little finger, had a smaller version of it made for her, declaring it to be the *real* ring (the parable of the ring) because everyone loved her so. Everything is made to point to the author of this *history*, the one and only suitable wooer for the grand-daughter of the old exegetist, of whom Freud sets out to be the inheritor (as of the other uncles as well) in July 1882. And now the message from the ancestor, Isaac B.:

The Jew, he said, is the highest pinnacle of humanity and created for pleasure. He despises all who are unable to enjoy things. (I had to think of what Eli [Martha's brother whom the prudent Freud never forgets] betrayed of his world view – to his credit, while intoxicated: Homo sum.) The law requires that the Jew takes delight in even the smallest pleasures, speaks the broche [= blessing] over every fruit, which reminds him of the connection with the beautiful world in which it has grown. The Jew upholds joy, and joy is made for the Jew. The teacher explained this with reference to the climax of the celebrations . . .

– that is the law for 'the *male* Jew'. Freud assures his bride that Freud* is also good for the *female* Jew and precisely *this* female Jew for him.

A customer came and Nathan was the salesman once more. I bade farewell with more emotion than the old Jew could have suspected. If he happens to visit Prague he will grant himself the pleasure of paying me a visit. He won't find me in Prague, but by way of substitute I shall –

he hasn't invented this old man. The old man who helps him devise the door-sign that is to hang above the entrance to the marriage between Bernays and Freud. Closing sentence:

---

*By adding an 'e', the name Freud becomes the German word for *joy*. (Trans.)

And when it comes to the two of us I think: even if the form in which the old Jews once felt content no longer provides us with shelter, something of its core, the essence of intelligent and cheerful Judaism, will not leave our house.

– a pretty door sign for love, no question about it. The joy given by the orthodox religion is to merge with the couple's worldly pleasure; and this generous letter is anything but miserly with the literal meaning of its author's name: there are not many texts in which Freud emblazoned the missing 'e' so clearly.

Emblazoned on the coat of arms for M & S. The letters continue for four years. They talk about everything that takes Freud's interest and use Martha as the focus for a body of writing which is on its way to finding itself and which *does* find itself. In writing the letters to his bride, Freud becomes an *author*, as did Kafka in his letters to Felice Bauer. They are the record of Freud's first attempts at psychoanalysis.

Drawing on Ernst Kris, the first editor of and commentator on Freud's later letters to Fließ, it has been frequently asserted that Fließ, as the recipient of these letters, had the function for Freud of an analyst from afar. What in the analytic situation was later termed 'transference' developed here between Freud and Fließ.

Fließ strikes me as something else: as that second partner who, as part of a productive 'male couple', was necessary to the development of psychoanalysis; a couple in which, after a period of collaboration, Freud gained the upper hand and then *consciously* pressed home a victory. But it is my belief that the letters written to Martha Bernays during their engagement had just such a function for Freud; at any rate, while reading them they struck me as the earliest (and sometimes surprisingly far-reaching) stage of the method of 'psychoanalysis'.

I would like to refer especially to the long letter to Martha of 2 February 1886 – it is too long to quote here – in which Freud analysed himself to Martha; the letter is very similar to what later will be called the record of an analytic session.

I think it is of significance for both Freud the person and the development of psychoanalysis that its earliest discovery occurs – as it were – in a love letter.

In this letter Freud reveals to Martha, among other things, that the 'mild neurasthenia' from which he constantly suffers always disappeared as if by magic when I was with you.

Martha, his love for Martha, his letters about his love for Martha, becomes a means for Freud to eliminate neurotic traits; writing to one's bride about one's love for her heals neuroses, says Freud.

The letter also mentions the sexual abstinence which Freud seems to have maintained during these years (which later corresponds with his wish that the patient should forgo 'sexual enactment', which disrupts analytic work).

Freud was working, especially in his letters from Paris, at transforming the engagement into a psychoanalysis, at transforming the stream of letters into the nascent form of self-analysis with the help of his fiancée as transference figure.

Martha becomes the preliminary sketch of an analytic authority without realizing. It would be exaggerated perhaps to say that Freud fulfilled his wish of marrying his analyst (before analysts existed, and thus rules to prevent this from happening), but it is not completely senseless.

The programme he sketched out for Martha and himself in his letters provides first of all for a substitution for his own family history, its *improvement* through Martha's relatives: these are quite different *paternal uncles* to the jailbird Uncle Josef with his forged roubles (as he keeps appearing, in cryptic form, in the *Interpretation of Dreams*); a different brother, Eli, who looks after the Bernays family more reputably than his own older brothers, with their dubious deals in Manchester, who also take care of 'the family' but do so probably with forged money and credit papers. An ideal brother, ideal uncle, just as one's heart desires: useful for both writing strategies and developing one's own person.

Second, Martha's father is a more upstanding businessman than his own father Jacob; a father, moreover, who is no longer alive: the position of father of the Bernays family is semi-vacant (offers room for personal expansion) but, perhaps even more important, it offers what may paradoxically be termed 'the missing handicap'. It is one thing to receive a wife from a father's hand and another to conquer her while side-stepping such a position of power. Freud frequently describes himself in his letters to Martha as a rebellious pupil, as the type of person who opposes the most various authorities. Now an adventurous gambler or revolutionary always becomes apparent (at least in the eyes of fathers with daughters to give away) in rebellious sons (-in-law), whom one may entrust with everything 'in life' (except just one thing): responsibility. But this is involved in giving away daughters.

In all probability *object-choice on the basis that the bride's father is missing* quite often plays a role in intensifying the affects of the man who has fallen in love.

Third, there is also the old Jew Isaac/Nathan Bernays, through whom Freud can draw on a kind of Jewish scholarly tradition which has been abandoned in his own family, or was never present in that way; in addition there is the link between this tradition and Western-Hamburg rationalism à la Lessing.*

That's a nicely wrapped bundle to dangle in front of the donkey in oneself and ensure that it takes a few steps, moves a bit more briskly, for Freud constantly has the feeling that he isn't working enough; of being rather a lazy person: he is already 26 and so remote from the marble bust he pictured of himself since the age of 16 or 17; he needs fire. This object-choice provides a lot of fire, and it keeps burning for a long time.

Incidentally, there can never be enough determinations: the maiden name of Martha's mother, Emmeline Bernays, is *Philipp*; so apart from everything else, Martha is also a *legitimate* Philipp

---

*Old Isaac Bernays certainly did have something of Nathan about him. After studying the Talmud, he read philosophy at the University of Würzburg; instead of the title 'Rabbi' he assumed the Portuguese title 'Chacam' (wise man), and he was the first orthodox Jew in Hamburg to preach in German (at the Kohlhöfen synagogue, until his death in 1849).

daughter. Freud had two older brothers from the first marriage of his father Jacob. They were both of marriageable age when Freud was a child. One of them, Philipp, lived unmarried in Jacob's household; he was the same age as Amalia, Freud's mother, and the father/husband Jacob Freud was often away from home for months on end (conveying textiles from Galicia to Bohemia). In the *Interpretation of Dreams* and many of Freud's letters his sister Anna appears as a Philipp daughter (not Jacob daughter). Curious birds from the Philippson's Bible, from which Sigmund Freud had learned to read as a child, appear (in Freud's dreams, which he reports and analyses) by night in his home and visit his mother Amalia ...

Presumably as a child Freud had seen his older brother Philipp with his mother (to whom the latter was not related). The rupture in the Freud family in 1860 – the older brothers went to England, the rest of the family to Vienna – probably resulted from this constellation (as is suggested by research like that of Marianne Krüll into Freud's childhood in Freiberg). This break and move to Vienna was decisive for the path Freud was later to take, on which he grants himself the pleasure, as we may put it, of finding a legitimate Philipp daughter and so inventing a further suitable constellation for eliminating a *blemish* in Freud's family novel. Martha is a very fruitful bride for diverse aspects of Freud's life plans.

Later the psychoanalyst Freud coins a term for such multiple interwoven and secured chains: overdetermination. Overdetermination in the development of symptoms, in the encoding of dream images ... in the construction of the loved one. Martha Bernays is married like an overdetermined symptom: symptom of a restoration of the groom's 'ability to work and love', guarantor of a re-editing of his personal history, overdetermined helper in a process of growth.

Freud's planning eye, which devises the Martha of his desires out of his need for a particular 'Martha', does not fall short of the *magnanimity of the engraver* in the entwinement of the M & S sign. His letters are addressed equally to the imaginary location of this *mutual entwinement* and the woman whom he sees at the side of the person he will one day become, as to the (more substantial) fiancée Martha and analyst Martha.

At this point we should stop at least briefly to remember the actual mother of the invention *the letters to the bride*: Emmeline Philipp-Bernays, Martha's mother. She was against the marriage between her daughter and the callow university doctor and abducted the former to Wandsbek until the latter attained the (economic) eligibility for marriage (and had perhaps forgotten the bride). But he did not 'forget' her in the least.

It seems that the process functions as *love* just as long as all options remain open; as long as Martha seems to be the woman who one day will exchange the notepaper for the paper of literary (or analytic) manuscripts; as long as something can be found in her replies (to Freudian inventions) that is necessary to the functioning of an 'analytic ear'; as long as there is written communication with ideal uncles, etc.

Freud writes programmatic letters 'to the bride' so that she will join in the game of his desire to (mutually) invent a woman who will wish to take active part (not only in the forthcoming production of children) in his work, his designs, his transformation from Freud into FREUD. The artistically entwined monogram of their initials should be seen less as the anticipation of child-producing love than as that other sort of LOVE which wishes to produce, give birth to something out of one's own wife, in this case a 'woman author' (in other cases another medial woman).

Freud's choice is tactical and strategic, as if it had been taken from a book (the *Book of Kings* in this case). It is executed with great circumspection and elegance, and makes some very skilled object-choice strategists look pretty pale by comparison.

There is a lovely passage in Freud's letters to Martha in which he emphasizes, during a masterly digression on an *other* possible object-choice, how familiar he is with the interlacing of love-choice and strategic calculation. In 1886, the last year of their engagement, Freud attended Charcot's lectures in Paris in order to learn his methods for treating hysterics. He was invited on several occasions to Charcot's home, and wrote to Martha on 20 January about the latter's family:

Madame is small, chubby, lively, has white powdered hair, is warm-hearted and not particularly distinguished in appearance. Their wealth comes from her, Charcot was a poor devil whilst her father apparently has countless millions. Mlle Jeanne Charcot is quite different, also small, quite buxom and almost comically similar in appearance to her ingenious father, and consequently so interesting, that one cannot stop to think whether she is pretty or not. She is about twenty, very natural and sociable. I hardly spoke with her because I remained with the old men, but R. talked to her a lot. Apparently she understands English and German. Just imagine: what a great temptation that would be if I were not already in love and otherwise an out-and-out adventurer. For nothing is more dangerous than a young woman who has the character-istics of a man one admires. I would be laughed at and thrown out, and be richer by a fine adventure. But it is better the way it is . . .

Martha must have written a few jealous words in response to this playfully presented version of the object-choice 'boss's daughter' (and she's rich too . . .), i.e. she played along; after a further visit to the Charcots, Freud brings the matter to a conclusion on 2 February with the words:

Mlle, who was wearing a Grecian costume and actually looked rather fetching – I can tell you this because your jealousy won't have lasted that long – shook me by the hand as I arrived but otherwise did not speak a word to me.

– but the word that one cannot stop to consider – whether daughters who come from the right men's hands are 'pretty' or not – has been spoken. The attractiveness of the bride is, in the right circumstances, a function of encoding male hands. We have already seen the work Sigmund did to equip Martha with the correct codes. Impressive.

... *you will call*

*

Later on, Martha Freud did not fulfil, or only partly, Freud's desire to make something different of her than what she probably was. Perhaps that is one of the reasons why Freud no longer recalls, or wishes to recall, his own particular type of object-choice 30 years later, when he is considering the mechanisms of falling in love. His love-choice of Martha Bernays was accompanied by disappointments.

She has neither become the writer he wanted (which is also hardly conceivable, given the 6 children she brought to the world during the first 9 years of marriage), nor, which is more serious for the development of their relationship, does she seem to have shown any lasting interest in the progress of Freud's work, 'psychoanalysis'.

This is apparent from various comments made by Freud, most noticeably in a letter to Fließ dated 8 February 1897. Freud would like to know whether Fließ has noted at what point little children begin to feel revulsion, and whether there is a period when they are very small in which they are free of revulsion. Why don't I myself go into the nursery and ... perform experiments? Because I don't have the time for it, what with working 12½ hours every day and the lack of support the womenfolk give me in my research.

The *womenfolk* are Martha Freud and her sister Minna Bernays, 4 years her junior, who, after the dissolution of her engagement with Ignaz Schönberg (a friend of Freud's who was dying of tuberculosis) by the latter himself, had moved into the Freuds' home during the 1890s and now helps Martha rear the many children.

At some stage of her life with Sigmund, Martha must have withdrawn her interest in Freud's 'analysing': not with the children, dear Sigmund; – a division of the spheres of influence in the home at Berggasse 19 between Freud-womenfolk and Freud-husband.

So Sigmund Freud, father of 6 (Anna, the youngest, is just 15 months old), has to ask Wilhelm Fließ in Berlin, father of 2, whose wife Ida shares his enthusiasm for observing children, about child behaviour. That is bitterly disappointing for a theoretician of early childhood sexuality, especially because there was no possibility of relying on any other clinical research.

Love in institutes (2): the intellectual sequences.

Freud did not simply resign himself to the withdrawal of interest in his researches from the women with whom he lived: other women took over this task, as and when this was possible; this was in some respects very simple, in others very difficult. Easy because, for instance, the female patients who came to him and remained generally had a burning interest in his system of treating neuroses with beautiful words; for an approach to their mental afflictions and finer mental points which had more to do with literature and play than conventional medicine. Obviously this exerted an enormous attraction and it is not difficult to imagine how Freud managed in this way to create an increasing number of female analysts; managing to turn the treatment into a training method and patients into informants and helpers in the expansion of psychoanalysis.

His relations with these women, who were rather like counterparts to his own wife at home, were difficult, however, because they could be nothing but close – and how was was he to deal with that?

Freud solved the problem in the long term by means of institutionalization: by setting up certain rules for relations between men and women who become members of the Psychoanalytic Association.

On the personal level this led to something akin to a sequence (a sequence that is very similar to the one I have described for art producers and their respective 'medial women').

These women, says Jones, had no erotic attraction for Freud. That is certainly not the case: it would be more correct to say that the erotic attraction was transformed, consciously and with great effort, into another form of affect, into a love of the collaboration on the development and establishment of psychoanalysis.

The most important was first of all his sister-in-law, Minna Bernays [says

Jones; but that was true, if at all, for only a short period], then in chronological order: Emma Eckstein, Loe Kann, Lou Andreas-Salomé, Joan Riviere, Marie Bonaparte.

The list is not complete, nor is that important here. What is important is the character of the 'sequence'. (Also interesting is the origin of this sequence; in all probability it does not go back to a woman [sister or mother] from Freud's own family, but rather to his nanny, Monika Zajìc, that ugly but clever old woman who taught young Sigmund to have a 'high opinion of himself' and whose resurrection in Freud's dreams in 1897 paved the way for the decisive step in developing the interpretation of dreams into an analytic procedure.)

One could say that during 1897, Shakespeare, Goethe, the railway, Freud's mother 'nudam' and Monika Zajìc all competed fiercely in Freud's dreams over who would provide the decisive impulse for the 'interpretation of dreams', and that Monika Zajìc won. (That just by the way.)

'Leaning' on her, on this cleverer-than-the-mother-was nanny, not only did an analytic interpretative procedure come into being but so, too, did a sequence-forming type of object-choice which clearly differed from the love-choice 'Martha'.

So do the numerous souls within one breast each develop their own object-choice? Apart from the type of man who falls in love with the 'same' woman, loses and finds her once again 20 times over, is there also a type who seeks another (or different sort of) lover for each of his egos or partial egos? (Which does not necessarily mean that one sort is 'relinquished' for the other.) A great deal depends on successful institutionalization.

Freud. Jung. Spielrein.
Struggle over an unborn child.

For thousands of years, institution-men (statesmen, church men, military men, lawyers, philosophers) have shown an undiminished concern for the fate of the unborn child. For the last couple of hundred years doctors and medicine men too.

If they had a completely free hand in establishing *their* version of the abortion law, the children would be brought to *the world* in the depot, or in the correct church, rough-hewn and ready to receive the fine polish for the respective needy institute, the army, the thinker's tower or whatever. But for all their efforts they are still not God, for it is women who give birth to the babies (= generate life; which, according to the evergreen best-seller of the institution-man breed, can only be done by a lord, *the* Lord).

From Plato, who places the responsibility for how and as what children enter this world from the OTHER on lots drawn in the beyond, to the Heidegger-lord who lets them be thrown into the hard bed of the modern world by the gender that is forever being left out, they do not slacken in proclaiming the law that it is they who *create* (the person as workhorse, as part of an institution). They themselves construct the female bodies they require (as country/ nation, Mother of God, birth-machine militia, Alma Mater or belly of the factory); and just the other day Mister Augstein* stuck a Pan-Germanic goddess on the cover of *Spiegel*. The men fight tooth and nail over the German spawn that is expected from the nether regions of reassembled Frau Germania.

Even in the life of Freud (who with Nietzsche and a couple of others is one of the few men to have had few doubts that it is women who create life) there was a similar moment of struggle over an unborn child. Inevitably it occurred during the expansion of psychoanalysis from a method for life, love and treatment into an institution, the International Psychoanalytic Association, which essentially took place between 1906 and 1913. The mother of the unborn child is the psychoanalyst Sabina Spielrein, and the paternity of the child is contested by Freud and his Swiss colleague C.G. Jung; neither of them is the physical father. But the child's mother is a daughter of the Psychoanalytic Association, and not just

---

*Rudolf Augstein, editor of the weekly current affairs magazine *Der Spiegel*. (Trans.)

. . . to endorse the reincarnation of – .

any daughter, but rather *the* founding daughter of the Association – and this is how it happened:

During the opening years of this century, Carl Gustav Jung, assistant doctor at the Burghölzli psychiatric hospital in Zurich, one of the Meccas of psychiatry at the time, converted to Freudian psychoanalysis (he became a passionate reader of the *Interpretation of Dreams*) and established contact. Freud was a Jewish-Austrian neurologist/psychiatrist who wrote little-read books (less than 1000 copies of the *Interpretation of Dreams* sold in the first few years); he was approaching fifty, had attained an associate professorship with great difficulty, but had the certainty of having recently discovered 'psychoanalysis'. His main problem was one of dissemination – friends and helpers in other towns and institutes. Burghölzli was a powerful institute. Carl Gustav Jung's letter arrived like a gift from so-called heaven. Freud made good use of this gift. Institutionalized psychoanalysis was built on the coalition with Burghölzli, whose director, Eugen Bleuler, also joined the newly inaugurated Association after a period of hesitation.

Freud knew that as an obscure Jewish interpreter of dreams from Vienna he would never succeed in establishing psychoanalysis in Western medicine without powerful institutional allies (the fact that he managed it at all is one of the wonders of the century). In the years that followed he called Bughölzli in Zurich his 'Aryan leg' because of its importance for the spread of psychoanalysis. Psychoanalysis could never have supported itself on one Jewish leg alone, let alone learnt to walk.

Sabina Spielrein, a Russian Jew from Rostov, had arrived in Burghölzli with the symptoms of a 'hysteric', and was the first female patient whom Jung decided to treat according to Freud's principles – more or less Jung's training case; but not simply Jung's training case, for it also became Sabine Spielrein's training analysis.

As with so many intellectual women during the beginnings of psychoanalysis, she fell passionately in love with the procedure and, together with Jung, was soon on the way to becoming an analyst.

It was supposed to go according to Freud's principles and then it didn't. Jung assumed the right in his very first analysis to violate the principle of the ban on love between analyst and patient. Without further ado, Spielrein and Jung turned the transference love, which, for Freud, necessarily develops at a certain point in the analytic cure, into a sexual one, and, in the exuberance of their feelings, intoxicated and transported by the new art (of loving) called psychoanalysis, believed they were precisely the two people – *the* analytic founding couple – from whom (he felt himself Goetheian, she more Nietzschean-superhuman, and both together Freudian) the psychoanalytic superman would arise; they called their eagerly awaited child 'the psychoanalytic Siegfried' (this was before Germany's two great Nibelung eras; the name is perhaps excusable, if you like).

Frau Spielrein allowed her imagination to take the relationship to its logical conclusions, she wanted to become Mrs Sabina Jung. Jung was married and, once his initial ardour had cooled (like Heidegger's for Hannah Arendt), did not wish to give up his marriage. There followed imbroglios, entanglements, gossip in Zurich; the arrival of Mrs Spielrein's parents who threatened Jung with legal action; I shall pass over the details of the unavoidable breach – but not that Jung, in his fix, sank so low as to have the cheek to invoice her for treatment and training sessions that had been spent in love-making.

She was, of course, systematically planning my seduction.... Now she is seeking revenge, Jung (seduced novice) complained to Freud in a letter of 4 June 1909.* Freud knew about this relationship very early on. Jung had informed him and asked for his advice. In his *own* fix (because of the 'Aryan leg'), Freud was unable to withdraw

---

*When, many years later, Jung found himself once again in the same constellation, and decided to live with both women in semi-marriage, he had learnt his lesson and came up with a psychological principle for each of them (like the 'Carl' and 'Gustav' in himself), Anima and one other. He taught as much in his books and proceeded to live with the two of them.

... they both have caused my heart to bleed.

from Jung the licence he was allowing to emerge. Like Groß*, she is a case of the struggle against the father which I wanted, in the Devil's name and with untold tons of patience, to cure gratissime (!), and even abused our friendship for that purpose, wrote Jung. Instead of giving him something to chew on (among other things on account of his syntax), Freud confirmed the existence of carefully planned seduction initiated by certain women among his own clientele: The way these women manage to charm us with every conceivable psychic perfection, until they have attained their purpose, is one of nature's greatest spectacles.... I myself have never fallen for it quite so badly, but I came very close on several occasions and had a narrow escape. In addition, adds Freud, he had been 10 years older than Jung is now, and thus more immune to the psychic perfections of woman. Then, summarizing:

But it does not do any harm. One simply develops the necessary thick skin, comes to master the 'countertransference', which we have to go through every time, and learns to displace one's own affects and deploy them to best advantage. It is a 'blessing in disguise'. (7 June 1909)

– the blessings come disguised. (The beauties of such didactic dramas during the analyst's training also remain concealed.) That just by the way.

More interesting here is the emphasis placed once again on displacing-and-expediently-deploying one's own affects: that seems to be the fate of LOVE once the first storm is over ... recognition after misperception ... (within and without the analyses) ... displacements, goals, placements ... life rewrites affects as effects.

Under the pressure of these 'affairs', Freud is compelled to write a closer account of 'countertransference'. This is not the only

---

*Otto Groß (1877–1920), anarchist and *enfant terrible* of psychoanalysis whose acknowledgement of the social dimension of neurosis clearly pre-dates Wilhelm Reich's (indeed that of Freud and Jung). Groß went to Burghölzli hospital in 1907 to cure his morphine and cocaine addiction, whereupon Jung saw fit to treat his colleague and friend's 'father complex' using psychoanalytic methods. After a few short weeks of truly epic analytic sessions, Groß fled, leaving Jung embarrassed and needing to justify his failure to his own 'father', Sigmund Freud. (Trans.)

psychoanalytic concept closely linked to the existence of Frau Spielrein.

Even after breaking with her, Jung did not stop torpedoing Freud's constructs of the analysis, and major Freudian concepts, both in theory and practice. By 1911 he had advanced to attacking Freud's central concept, the libido. This finally led to the split between Freud and Jung, which I will come to shortly.

Now a psychoanalyst in her own right, Sabina Spielrein moves to Vienna during the disputes with Jung and the shifts in power at the centre of the Psychoanalytic Association, and participates regularly in Freud's Wednesday gatherings. The records show that Freud was unable to avoid criticizing certain Zurich undertones in his young colleague's comments; but now it is criticism among friends. Sabina Spielrein is a highly regarded member of the Viennese Association who writes articles in the psychoanalytic journals, while Jung – the fronts have reversed – has changed to the position of the Devil who is damaging psychoanalysis in public.

Sabina Spielrein marries the Russian-Jewish physician Dr Pawel Scheftel in 1912. In 1913 she is pregnant. There are no doubts about the child's paternity. But (in Freud's eyes) something seems to have been missing in *the blessing* on this constellation: Spielrein had never openly 'renounced' (or whatever one calls it) her relationship with Jung; on the contrary. She had toppled the analyst, her former lover, but kept a memento (or whatever one calls it). Freud felt himself compelled ('battle over daughters' body territories'; 'struggle for the unborn children') to write her a letter in August 1913 during the summer vacation. It ran:

I cannot stand it when you still enthuse about your old love and past ideals, and reckon with a confederate in the form of the great, tiny, unknown [= the unborn child].

As you know, I myself have overcome every trace of my love of Aryanism and hope to presume that, if it is a boy, it shall develop into a sturdy Zionist.

He or she must be black at any rate [black like love], no more blonds, let's have done with these will-o'-the-wisps!

I will not give Jung your regards in Munich, you know that. But you I wish all the best, and a surplus of tenderness, humour and understanding so that there will be more than enough to pass on to the young little life.

We are Jews and will remain so. The others will always only exploit us and never understand or appreciate what we do.

With my warmest greetings
Yours, Freud

'What, did Freud write that?!' I hear someone ask every time I read this out; that doesn't *sound* like him. Is it that bad? Yes and no. Apart from the better side of the letter – that a Jew can give vent to his rage at those so-called 'Aryan' idiots – there is the truly lamentable occupation of this baby and the reclamation of this daughter's body 'for himself'.

The declared and genuine anti-racist Freud is unable to avoid detecting, as analyst/Jew/institution founder, a Jewish daughter in the pregnant body of a woman who belongs to his institution, and (as patriarch of the institution) expropriating the unborn child in order to score a victory over the enemy institution-man/Aryan: Jung. He cannot stop fighting Jung on a territory that belongs even less to him than it does to Jung: Jung at least had once been allowed access to it. Freud's anti-Nibelung attack does not even have Sabina Spielrein as an ally: her body is the *terrain* over which the battle (the love . . .) is being fought.

Finally Sabina Spielrein gave birth to a girl, and Freud wrote:

Dear Doctor Spielrein

Allow me to send you my heartfelt congratulations! It is better that it is a 'she'. One can still think about the blond Siegfried, and perhaps have destroyed an idol before his time comes. Incidentally the little She will be able to speak for herself. May she prosper, if wishes still have any remnant of their omnipotence!

Yours, Freud

– did *Freud* write that? That's (just) how one writes when the omnipotence of one's wishes (i.e. wishing to get rid of others and to be oneself the *spiritual* father of all the children of all women for whom one believes this necessary for reasons of medial control and disputed allegiance) fails. Freud turns himself into the racially correct institutional father of the newly born Renate Spielrein, without even mentioning the real Jewish father, but making of the baby a weapon to 'destroy an idol'.

That's crucial in the institutional economy of kings: holding control of all the daughters in one's kingdom who are already born or about to be born, whether they are blessed with bountiful intelligence, a good analytic ear, a beautiful singing voice, dextrous fingers, nimble dancing legs, or skilled in some technical procedure or other. Anyone who fails to colonize enough daughters, or to turn able women and potential 'lovers' into medial women or organization daughters, will fail to extend his kingdoms. (Although colonizing can also mean snatching 'the daughters' from the clutches of worse despots; 'liberating' them.)

There has been no more liberating organization for women this century than psychoanalysis, their daughter state.

But there were despotic letters to women like Sabina Spielrein in 1913/14. Freud could not have written such letters every year of his life. They were not in keeping with his 'character', originating rather in constellations – of power, confederacy and love and of the sexes in an institution.

The threshold of the First World War was also the darkest year in the battle for survival of psychoanalysis: just in the process of becoming a world-wide network, it might have torn apart ... would the programme keep going without the power of the Zurich transmitter ... also without the Adlerian wing which was breaking away from the Association in Vienna at the same time ... would the other chapters remain ... Berlin ... New York ... London ... or align themselves with Jung ... follow Hirschfeld ... would the newly founded periodicals be able to keep going ... or would the editors change sides ... flags flying ... and thus *aquis submersus* psychoanalysis, not exactly *culpa patris*, but through the fault of one of the

. . . at my window with a broken wing.

fathers? . . . Freud wanted to avoid that.

Sabina Spielrein, hotly contested daughter-territory of two founding heroes, spoke out in full knowledge of this status. In terms of allegiance, she decided openly for Freud's state; on the 'personal' level, however, while distinguishing clearly between Freud's and Jung's positions in her genealogy, she attempted to make both members of her psycho-family. She writes to Freud in 1914:

I was even less able to forgive J.[ung]'s attitude to our [psychoanalytic] Association than I was in my own private matter. I only saw him once after my marriage, but in the end I am not the father, but rather the sister.

(That is, I am not Freud, so I cannot act as *father* and put Jung in his place.) She continues:

For all his errors, I am still fond of J. [fond that is in a psycho-sisterly way] and would like to bring him back to us. Neither you, *dear Professor*, nor he realize that the two of you belong together far more closely than anyone could imagine. But this devout wish is not a betrayal of our Association!

What we read here is the daughterly wish that the war between two kings should not be a fight to the finish; it would wound *her*. She wants two sorts of king: a father king and a brother king; she herself as their daughter/sister in the psychoanalytic state – incidentally 'Siegfried' was a child born of *a brother and sister*, the royal children Siegmund and Sieglinde.

Jung as former loved one (*the* love), and herself as former lover, are eliminated from the arrangement (inasmuch as she herself is not involved as *current* wife and mother). Order reigns over the spheres of production. (Chasms.)

Institutional love (3): Spiritual brides.

In order to restructure the different kinds of love in the analytic process into an institutionalized love of work, a procedure was developed which turned admittance to the psychoanalytic institution into something like the admittance to an order. With this, love in this institution becomes comparable to the institutional love which the members of other, for example, religious, orders show the figure of their spiritual master. Quite a number of women analysts have seen themselves as Freud's spiritual brides, and not only in the early years. This spiritual love radiates, undisguised, at appropriate times and places among members of the analytical daughterhood to the present day. They show a sort of pride in this love.

Freud was one of those clever state founders who know that 'spiritual masters' who lack sufficient property or enough credit from the bank, and have to prop up their realm on the wealth of human bodies (in this case the bodies of middle-class daughters emancipating themselves at the turn of the century), must provide these daughters with institutional protection against sexual approaches by 'the master' and his deputies.

This is not a matter of course in academic institutions, for example. Recently I heard a young woman professor from a Californian university express thanks in public for being lucky enough not to have had to sleep with *every* lord who was involved in her attaining her tenureship. In the end sexually despotic academic-primates drive 'the daughters' away.

In the more peaceable (state-founding) version of the paternal economy, the father allies himself with the daughters in a developmental-spiritual way, and not a despotic-sexual one. The daughters remain at his *disposal* (in strong distinction to the old patriarchal form of marriage) as large, previously untapped sources of creative energy. In terms of social theory, the International Psychoanalytic Association established by Freud is a daughter state under male sovereignty.

The childlessness of a large number of women analysts to date might be regarded as a sign of this special daughter status. Childlessness (or restricting oneself to *one* child) is, however, imposed upon the majority of women who take/took up careers in academic life or in industry. But it has a particular significance in an institution whose fundamental principles include researching the development of young children. It would have been *logical* to encourage precisely women analysts to have children and to create suitable conditions for this in the institution. Another, stronger (institutional) logic conflicts with this.* Being the *daughter* of an institution (or rather priestess of a spiritual learning) is not easily compatible with maternal functions. I shall return to this later, in connection with Anna Freud.

So there are modes of loving, modes of marrying, modes of not marrying, modes of procreating or not procreating that are generated by certain institutions which ensure that love affects are not left to float freely, but are restructured, adjusted and harnessed to the institution. It creates ways of working, living and loving which above all transform the sexuality of its members into energies that keep the institution running (or 'feed it').

Freud and Emma Jung.
Messages in bottles in exceedingly deep waters.

How did Freud's real relations with women influence his theoretical constructions on object-choice? What connection was there between these women's relations with Freud and the four types of 'female object-choice' which Freud posited in his *narcissism text*?

Freud's relations with Emma Jung, the wife of Carl Gustav Jung, will be examined first before attempting an answer.

As the wife of the 'crown prince' (and passionate reader of Freud's texts), Emma Jung had a preset, institutional-familial

---

*It has also ensured that child analysis has never become an obligatory part of analytic training, although this would have been imperative from the vantage point of psychoanalytic theory.

relationship with Freud . . . there were exchanges of letters . . . visits . . . familial sympathy . . . interest in the growth of the 'Association' . . . interest in the friendship between the two founders. But was it actually *friendship*? Emma Jung must have been the first to notice as the relationship between the two men began to crumble. The moment she perceived this she seized the opportunity to alter her relationship with Freud. Stepping out of the shadow of the *male couple*, at first (still with reference to the two men) as a go-between, she revealed herself in a number of letters as a quite different figure, as a loving person with a special *understanding* of Freud, his situation, his age, his life circumstances.

I shall describe how Freud reacted to this.

In the early summer of 1911, Carl Gustav Jung had noted a few remarkable things while studying the night sky over Zurich (perhaps a few stars could still be spotted on which the great Freud had not *yet* written his name); they related to the *nature of the libido* and he passed them on to Vienna on 12 June 1911. Starting with *Dear Herr Professor!* Jung informed Freud that he had been able to determine exactly the 'mother complex' of the mother of one of his female patients (who also suffered from it) from certain positions of the stars. This opened up new perspectives to him:

I dare say that we may one day discover in astrology a good deal of knowledge that has been intuitively projected into the heavens. It seems, for instance, that the signs of the zodiac are character pictures, i.e. libido symbols which depict the typical libidinal properties in question.

In the long run, not even the best institutional legwork can side-step these sorts of blows to the substance of psychoanalysis, particularly as Jung began to publish much the same. (Adler, Stekel, Hitschmann, everyone *in Vienna* would have been kicked out of the door to Freud's psychoanalytic edifice ten times over if they had turned up with anything like that.)

The Zurich bonus still holds . . . but the beams are beginning to buckle.

There are also a couple of nice letters in the edition of the Jung–Freud correspondence; at least two. These are the ones that Emma Jung wrote at this time. They are very different from those of the men. She accomplishes something that the two of them had not managed in almost 300 letters over 5 years; to speak openly about the relationship between them.

Tactical introduction:

I'm not really sure how I have managed to pluck up the courage to write this letter to you, but I think I am safe in saying that it is not the result of 'presumption';* rather I am following the voice of my unconscious, which I have so often had to concede is right . . .

– it's best to approach Herr Professor with his favourite concept. But what she then writes is simply what she has seen and heard:

You see, since you visited us I have been tormented by the idea that your relationship with my husband is not altogether what it could or should be, and since that really ought not to be the case, I would like to try to do everything that is within my power. I don't know whether I am deceiving myself when I think that somehow you do not completely agree with the 'Transformations of the Libido'. You did not even mention it and yet I believe that it would do you both a lot of good if you would really speak your minds about it on some occasion. Or is something else the matter? If so please tell me what, dear Herr Professor; for I cannot bear to see you so resigned and I feel sure that your resignation is not simply concerned with your real children (I was really struck by the way you talked about it), but also with your spiritual sons; otherwise you would scarcely have any reason to be resigned.

So Carl Gustav Jung would in fact be a *real* reason, according to her. And Freud had not summoned up the courage to bring this up during his visit, but complained instead about certain developments in his *own* children.

---

*The word 'presumption' (*Übermut*; literally 'super-courage') echoes the word for 'courage' (*Mut*) in the original. (Trans.)

Please don't think of my course of action as meddlesome and do not place me with those women who, as you once said, always interfere in your friendships. Naturally my husband knows nothing of this letter and I beg you not to hold him responsible for it or let him bear the brunt of any unpleasant effects it may have on you.

In any case I hope that you will not be angry with your great admirer

Emma Jung (30 October 1911)

– she has stepped on to thin ice. But since Freud himself had broached the subject (in his eyes Mathilde Breuer and Ida Fließ were partly responsible for the breakdown in his collaboration with the two men), it held. Risky, furthermore, are her references to Freud's 'own' and 'spiritual' sons; Freud's 'resignation'; Carl's libido deviation.

In a letter written at almost the same time, Freud writes to her husband saying that he feels rather grumpy and is physically in poor shape, and hopes that he isn't turning into a cantankerous old man, adding that such people deserve to be slain without remorse.

Emma's letter fell on fertile soil, the ice held, Freud sent a friendly reply and she felt encouraged to pursue the matter.

My dear Herr Professor,

Your nice kind letter has removed my uneasy doubts, for I began to feel afraid that in the end I had done something stupid [something like female anxiety No. 1; successfully drummed into her as well]. Naturally I feel very glad and thank you with all my heart for the friendly way you received my letter and above all for the affection that you show us all.... The reason I mentioned the 'Transformations' was mainly because I knew how eagerly Carl was waiting for your opinion; he had often said that he was sure you would not approve of it, and thus awaited your verdict with some trepidation.

– in his reply, Freud will turn this little betrayal of Carl into the reproach that *she* too is disrupting his male friendships.

I find it hard to believe ...

Of course it is just a remnant of the father (or mother) complex, which is presumably being resolved in this book; for actually Carl should not need to worry about the opinions of others if he holds something to be right. So perhaps it is all to the good that you did not respond at once, so as not to reinforce this father–son relationship.

– now the ice is really thin. She is talking as an interpreter, as Freud's equal.

The second reason was provided by our conversation on the first morning after your arrival, when you told me about your family [= without Carl]. You said then that your marriage [with Martha] had long since been amortized, and now there was nothing left to do except – die. And that one rears one's children until they are grown up, and with that they really start to become a worry, and yet that is the only true joy. This made such an impression on me and seemed to be of such importance that I had to keep thinking of it and I fancied that it was addressed only to me, because at the same time it was also meant symbolically and referred to my husband.

Please don't be angry if I* venture also to speak about the 'manifest content' of what you said. I wanted to ask at the time whether you are sure that your children could not be helped by analysis. One certainly cannot be the child of a great man with impunity, considering the trouble one has in making the break with ordinary fathers. And when this distinguished father also has a streak of patriarchism in him, as you yourself said! Didn't the fracture of your son's leg also fit into this picture? [Wow!] When I tried to enquire about it you answered that you did not have the time to analyse your children's dreams because you had to earn money so that they could carry on dreaming. Do you think that this attitude is right? I would have thought rather that one *should not* dream at all, but live instead [– 'the Jew upholds joy, and joy is made

---

*In the published edition of the letters, the word 'I' has been inserted in square brackets by the editor. Emma Jung's analytic hand had not dared to write the word 'I' at this point.

for the Jew']. I have also found with Carl that the imperative 'earn money' is only a way of evading something to which he has resistances. Please excuse my openness, which perhaps will seem impudent to you; but it spoils my picture of you because somehow I can't make it rhyme with the rest of your nature, and that is so important to me. The thought even occurred to me that perhaps you didn't send your son to study in Zurich on account of us; you did speak of it once, and naturally we would have been delighted to see him from time to time.

Another thing I must also mention is your resignation with regard to science, if one may put it that way. I am sure you can imagine how pleased and honoured I am by the confidence you have in Carl, but sometimes it almost seems to me as though you were bestowing too much on him; do you not see in him your successor and fulfiller more than you need? Doesn't one often give much because one wishes to keep much?

Why are you already thinking of ceding instead of enjoying your well-earned fame and success? Perhaps so that you will not miss the right moment? That will certainly never happen to *you*. You are far from being old enough to start talking about the 'path of regression', what with all those wonderful and fruitful ideas you have in your head! Besides, anyone who could discover the living fountain of the PsA [psychoanalysis] (or do you not believe that it is one?) will not grow old that quickly [that must have pierced him to the heart].

No, you should be glad and enjoy the pleasures of the victor after having struggled for so long. And do not think of Carl with a father's feelings: 'He will grow but I must wane,' but rather as one person thinks of another who, like you, has his own law to fulfil.

Don't be angry.
Yours, with my warmest love and admiration
Emma Jung (6 November 1911)

Freud was unable to accept this lesson in psychoanalysis and clear letter writing, delivered in a spirit of affection. She had overstepped the mark.

This female voice enters the lives of a great many men at some time and place, mostly from very *close quarters*, telling a truth, truth based on keen observations; the same truth that rings from Else Lasker-Schüler's messages in bottles which Benn allowed to float past* on his way to the top. The men with artillery shells ringing in their ears, with the detonations of wars in which they are caught up, and deaf from the echo of their own contributions, are unable to hear such words.

What is occurring between her husband and Freud, her husband and her and her and Freud, between the two men and the Association they chair: that Freud would have to compensate for an 'amortized marriage' (strange the 'amor' in this word) with the further development of psychoanalysis, if this marriage could not be restored, instead of with anxieties about his successor, instead of playing the ageing ruler in the fictive kingdom of the psycho-analysts who does not sleep at night for fear of the potential desires of his sons from the primal horde,** instead of the business with the libido concept, his own children breaking their legs; and that the pleasures of a 'victor' which deserved the name lie apparently in enjoyment (a long list of things which would have delighted Freud if he had said them himself).

This curious contradiction: on the one hand, saying that all that remained was death (as Freud said to the living Emma Jung), and, on the other, fighting tooth and nail over every inch of ground in the IPA, against 'deviations' in his friends' thinking . . . expulsions . . . coalitions . . .: the correspondence with Jung is excruciating to read, recording the intrigues behind the scenes for pages on end . . . paranoid Adler in Vienna . . . homosexual, unappetising Hirsch-feld in Berlin . . . all to the good if they leave –

– why bother when nothing but a (rather dreary) death is waiting at the end of an amortized life which one welcomes with 'resign-ation'? Why bother? The 'dear professor' is in need of a small

---

*Else Lasker-Schüler (1869–1945), the foremost female poet of Expressionism, was fervently admired by Benn, but he failed to hear her warnings about National Socialism (see *Orpheus and Eurydice*). (Trans.)

**Naturally, instead of sleeping at night, Freud works on *Totem and Taboo*, one of the texts accompanying the internal power struggles in the International Psycho-analytic Association. Anthropologists always found this text 'abysmal'.

injection of life – and, if it's needed and desired, then why not from her and through her: Emma Jung is not ashamed to be so open (she does not complain directly about Carl; she only does that in her next letter), but one senses that she is not acting as an agent for her husband's interests. The fear of losing Freud is more important to her than the fear that Carl is not being treated properly by Freud.

Emma Jung's intervention achieves the opposite of what she had intended. Freud distances himself rapidly (by letter) from her and moves closer to Carl Gustav. Luke-warm praise for *Symbols of Transformation* is passed his way – the best that the promising author has written to date, as Freud wrote to his friend six days after Emma's letter; not only telling an untruth, but also – with the words 'promising author' – tightening the father–son screw to an unbearable degree, just as Emma was trying to loosen it; but the split has been deferred for another two years.

She also receives a letter (which we only know about from her answer), and at the same time as Carl Gustav. The two of them, Carl and Emma, reply on the same day, 14 November, Carl at least knowing nothing of Emma's letter. A few of the things that Freud wrote can be gleaned from Emma Jung's answer.

Küsnach, 14 November 1911

Dear Herr Professor!
You certainly were annoyed by my letter, weren't you? As was I, but it has cured me now of my megalomania and makes me wonder just what devilment of my unconscious made you, of all people, the victim of this madness. And here I must confess, if very reluctantly, that you are right: my last letter, especially the tone of it, was actually directed to the father imago, to which one should of course demonstrate fearlessness.

– she had written to the father imago? Not with a single word, even if one reads the letter a hundred times, which is also why I have quoted it at such length: as object of this Freudian diagnosis that followed straight after. If it was directed at an 'imago', then it was at that of an admired friend or lover. It is not so surprising that the man concerned answers with *interpretations*; but Freud does more: he imputes what he himself has done in his letter to C.G. Jung, namely reinforcing and elevating his father imago, to Emma Jung – who was perhaps the only person at the time who did *not* address him in this role. He had encouraged her to ride across Lake Constance;* she had set off with a cheery *My* dear Herr Professor (which is now once again missing) and an opening comma after the address;** the ice held, there didn't even seem to be any ice. And now that she has ridden too close, he lets her fall through, and she (obediently) is full of regret, takes everything back ... back to the position of the daughter who is eager to learn and which she had *abandoned* ... another case of the *sorcerer's apprentice*, female version, November 1911:

After I had thought for so long before writing to you, and believed that I completely understood my motives, my unconscious has now played another trick on me after all, and a particularly subtle one: for I am sure you can imagine how delighted I am to make a fool of myself in front of you, of all people. I can only pray and hope that your judgement will not prove too severe.

– her cheeky head is laid upon the executioner's block of his concepts; and in Sigmund's hand the 'unconscious' turns into a magic wand; everything falls into its proper place. He must have bathed in the situation like Siegfried in dragon's blood. But Emma is no Kriemhild, who could send a Hagen with a linden leaf to the spot(s) she had seen.† *Mea Culpa* that I saw something, she says, but

---

*'The Rider and Lake Constance', a ballad by Gustav Schwab (1792–1850), tells of a horseman who sets out to visit Lake Constance: only when he suddenly discovers himself in Switzerland does he realize that he has been riding over the frozen waters, whereupon he falls from his horse, dead, into a convenient ditch! (Trans.)

**The formal address used in German letters ends with an exclamation mark, as in: Dear Herr Professor! (Trans.)

†In the *Song of the Nibelungs*, Siegfried made himself invincible by bathing in dragon's blood, but a linden leaf fell on his shoulder during the process and rendered him vulnerable in one spot. His wife Kriemhilde unwittingly betrayed this spot to Hagen, her servant, who imparted the knowledge to Brunhilde, thus enabling her to kill the hero. (Trans.)

... here's what you got to do. You got to –

in fact there was nothing. She also *missed the mark* with her comments on the relationship between the two men, and with other classical, perceptive phrases used by over-hasty analysands who have the cheek to offer an interpretation of the analyst.

I agree then that I have projected something from my immediate surroundings into distant Vienna, and am annoyed that one always sees what's closest to oneself in the worst light. You have also completely misunderstood my admittedly unwarranted intrusion on your family affairs. I really had no wish to cast a shadow on your children. I am fully aware that they have turned out fine and have never doubted this in the least. I hope you do not seriously believe that I intended to say that they are 'doomed to be degenerate' [– now that is a *quote* from Freud]. I did not write anything that could be understood even vaguely in that way. [– Nor had she; but she is standing with her back to every wall and is building bridges to the inadmissible idea that the physical illnesses of Freud's children might also be *psychically* determined: builds bridges with all that remains to her, her own neurotic body:] Since I have made some highly astonishing discoveries about myself in this respect and still do not consider myself particularly degenerate or exceptionally hysterical, I thought that similar phenomena are also possible in others [= exactly Freud's own procedure]. I would be grateful to you if you would set me right about that.

– Freud's letter must have been so fierce and aggressive that Emma Jung was unable to grasp it as anything but the (obligatory) reproach of hysteria addressed to disobedient or sexual women. *The Taming of the Shrew* keeps popping up somewhere or other in the repertory.

Soon Freud will write that the state of love/being in love is one of neurotic misperception. Emma Jung's letters in his drawer might have convinced him of the opposite: that loving sympathy and interest make for clear-sightedness.

Freud answered with interpretations and suspicions of hysteria; sobered, Emma Jung steps back into the *sequence of non-hysterical* pupils, back with a formulation which retains its eloquence and

77

truthfulness inasmuch as the sentences would be most apt as a preamble to the fundamental law that submission to the master ensures happiness:

I give you my heartfelt thanks that you consider it worthwhile to discuss your most personal affairs with me. What you say to me sounds so convincing that I have to believe it, even if something inside me still resists. But I have to admit that you have the experience and not I, and that consequently I am no longer able to give you any convincing replies. But you have recognized one thing quite correctly: that despite everything the whole matter is purely and simply a disguised homage whose clumsy costume you are willing to forgive.

What remains is the realization that she has been expelled once and for all from the male couple (cemented together with fake cement) Freud/Jung, and placed among the women who disrupt Freud's friendships. The last sentence of the letter:

Please don't write to Carl about any of this; I feel bad enough as it is.

Overcome by the sighs and moans from this little scrap of misery, Freud sends a dose of comfort, and is thanked by the recipient on 24 November:

My dear Herr Professor!
Heartfelt thanks for your letter. I can tell you to your relief that I am not always as despondent as I was in my last letter; I was afraid that you were angry with me or had a bad opinion of me, and that made me very downhearted, especially because you hit upon my central complex [= being despondent as a result of her own bad opinion of herself. But she merely had an excess of feelings in spots where men are mostly anaesthetic: in their self-perceptions and in their perception of their own independence from the love of others]. Usually I am quite at one with my fate and understand completely how lucky I am, but from time to time I am tormented by conflicts as to how I can make myself felt next to Carl; [now she's lying where she belongs, on a couch:] I feel that I do not have any friends, all the people who associate

with us want only to see Carl, apart from a few boring people whom I
find totally uninteresting.

Naturally the women are all in love with him, and I'm cut off in any case
from the men because I am the wife of the father [C.G. as the father of the
Zurich analysts] or of their friend. But I have a strong need for people, and
Carl also says that I shouldn't carry on concentrating solely on him and the
children, but how am I to accomplish that? It is very difficult given my
strong tendency towards autoeroticism, but it is certainly also objectively
difficult because I can never compete with Carl.

She makes the complaint that Carl has all the women of the
Association while she has only Carl, and Carl in fact doesn't have
her, or scarcely, because Carl is the person who does not maintain
the division between spiritual lovers and sexual lovers in his
daughter state, as Freud attempts to do. But she is taboo for other
men because she is the wife of the king (although she would not
necessarily be taboo for Freud). Freud had doubtless seen the
implication, it's there to be read, and the last of Emma Jung's
letters underlines it as sexual desire. I don't know any more about
the rest of her life in Zurich and so will leave a gap here.

It is possible that Freud had sensed this particular undertone in
Emma Jung's approaches all along and rejected it ('a Zurich
illness'). It is also possible that Emma Jung was in any case 'out of
the question' (on grounds of attachment . . . the wrong cheekbones
. . . wrong teeth). The last lines of this letter of Emma's prove, at any
rate, to be the last the two of them will exchange: Would you mind
advising me, dear Herr Professor, and if necessary even give me a little
reprimand? I am so grateful for your help and consideration. With
fondest regards . . . Freud didn't want to do that, didn't want to give
Emma advice on how to handle Carl Gustav's sexuality.

*

Emma Jung reverts to her place at the bottom of Freud's letters as
one of those to whom he asks to be remembered. Freud does not
want to produce or create anything with her. Her offer to turn him

from a paranoid-resigned ruler into one who can enjoy the fruits of his labours (and perhaps a new love) is quite consciously and emphatically refused in the letter he sends simultaneously to Carl Gustav Jung – making it clear who *the couple* is here and what sort of couple it is, namely one that is giving birth. And the two letters which Freud writes to Jung after Emma's lovely letter of 6 November (on 14 and 16 November) talk precisely about birth:

My dear friend

I am pleased to be able to tell you that yesterday the psa periodical [i.e. *Imago*] was finalized by myself, the editors Sachs and Rank and the publisher Heller in Vienna. The first issue should appear in the middle of March 1912. I am counting on your goodwill towards the newborn child, as well as your support. For it too belongs to the goods that some day I want to leave to you.

– the last sentence as an appeasement of Jung's (rightly) assumed jealousy, because Freud is associating with other partners in Vienna. Male-masculine production sexuality routs heterosexual seductions (especially relationships between masters and 'daughters').

Two days later he emphasizes the necessity of work on this birth and again appeases Jung, who has complained about Rank's promotion to editor (= competitor with Jung, who edits the *Jahrbuch*):

Rank's promotion to editor won't mean any loss to you. If he does anything purely psa, he will certainly send it to the *Jahrbuch*, and anyway you wouldn't have had enough room for his 'Lohengrin', for instance. Incidentally the *Jahrbuch*, *Zentralblatt* and the newly born child are not intended to be three separate individuals, but rather so many different organs in one biological individual.

– that is the answer that she (Emma reads Freud's letters to Carl with him) receives, via her husband: that she is not authorized to translate Freud's comment on his 'amortized marriage' to mean that he is looking for another woman or love; on the contrary, he is *very busy giving birth* to the various organs of a being which Freud (wiping away Emma's thoughts about the well- or ill-bred children he had with Martha) calls a *biological individual.* He has not *finished* with producing children and finding love partners. An analytical couple & 1 publisher in Vienna give birth to *Imago,* child of a *special* order. This woman from Küsnach who *jumps* from one order to the next, with whose husband, Dr Jung, he conceived and gave birth to the *Jahrbuch,* and whom he (himself *vacillating* slightly between the orders) allowed too much insight into his *other* life, is unable to see that these babies are starting to crawl very nicely, that *that* is the life which she missed in him.

Freud's 'libido' relates to objects of a *quite different* kind in quite different orders of life.

A decision based on love tactics: the children *Zentralblatt, Jahrbuch* and *Imago* must at least be out of the crawling stage before his love can be withdrawn from Jung, the most important co-mother.

Freud, 1914. 'On Narcissism: An Introduction'.
Four 'female' types of object-choice.

Freud's 1914 essay 'On Narcissism' is a curious hybrid when compared with his other texts; this is the consequence of the numerous functions which the text had to fulfil at the time of its publication. He does not limit himself, as in other texts, to the introduction of new specific concepts, or the extension of psycho-analytic theory and technique, but conducts a battle on several fronts.

It is the text that must respond to the split with the Zurich group around Jung and the departure from the IPA of the Viennese group around Adler, and at the same time is to save the libido concept, which Freud considers to be the heart of psychoanalysis, from Jung's attacks. Jung had written that it was widely known that the libido theory was untenable and that Freud himself had long since disassociated himself from it.

Freud denies this vehemently and counters with the introduction of a new concept, namely the primary narcissism of the small child, which in this context has the key function of bolstering up the 'libido' as the central concept of psychoanalysis.

The first part of the narcissism text is more or less a timely settling of accounts with the various mistakes made by all existing psychiatric tendencies, as well as with the errors of the currents in psychoanalysis that deviate from Freud's; extremely complicated and brilliantly fought (Freud accepts just one aide in this battle on all fronts: Sandor Ferenczi); apart from which he seeks victory by summoning a new figure from the wings; a figure he presents in this text as *His Majesty the Baby.* (Guardian of the almost lost treasure, the libido.)

This baby, with its 'primary narcissism', on the one hand, and its urge to repeat early experiences of satisfaction, on the other, governs the concept of love that Freud outlines in this text, in which he says that sexual instincts are derived from the instincts for self-preservation and only later become independent; there is no form of love that does not repeat infantile models; object-choice of the attachment type and object-choice of the narcissistic type describe precisely the two sides of his majesty's possible choice.

It's a matter of psychic cathectic energies. Infantile libido either cathects external objects or takes its own body as love object. With that a broad spectrum is covered, if not everything ('the world'); that is the aim of Freud's war here, and the 2 types of object-choice which he leads into battle suffice.

The war also has a number of secondary theatres, or, perhaps better, a number of hidden, not directly visible battle fields. When Freud says that he has discovered the narcissistic type of object-choice particularly among 'homosexuals and perverts', but without saying a word as to why and in what way their sort of object-choice should be viewed as 'narcissistic', he is referring to the completely unresolved debate about the links between paranoia and homosexuality (is President Schreber a repressed homosexual? Of what nature would his 'perversion' be otherwise? What sort of libido is at work in such cases? Jung had maintained that there are no sexual ones involved, etc.).

The NARCISSUS who is introduced to psychoanalytic theory in 'On Narcissism' has to work many fields, has to stand in for many figures and cracks in the system, and Freud is aware that he can neither fill all the joints nor buttress all of the collapsing walls. In this cavalry charge to save the libido and strategically correct his disloyal schools he lacks the peace of mind needed for the careful deployment of the new concept. The text is fighting for the theoretical and practical survival of psychoanalysis, for the main- tenance of the central analytic concepts (and in the background for the maintenance of the analytic institutions which have begun to form at various places around the world in the preceding years, bound together by the covers of the periodicals).

Accordingly, Freud relativizes his pronouncements: it is time once again to remind the adherents of psychoanalysis that all our provisional ideas in psychology will presumably some day be based on an organic substructure. This makes it probable that it is special substances and chemical processes which perform the operations of sexuality. . . . We are taking this probability into account in replacing the special chemical substances by special physical forces. (That love is a smell is demonstrated – time and again – by chemical experiments; it's not surprising; of course the various psycho-classes have their own respective chemistries, and attachment types know full well who gets up their nose and who doesn't; every dog smells a person's *psyche* from his sweat; but the chemistry of the *libido* still does not explain this.)

Substitutes/provisional ideas/certainties follow one another at a rapid pace. One paragraph repudiates or limits what the previous one has proposed, as when Freud negates the distinction he has just introduced between the various types of object-choice by inserting the sentence that both kinds of object-choice are open to each individual, though he may show a preference for one or the other. Once again, there is no justification for this later in the text. In the end, object-choice of the attachment type, autoerotic self-cathexis, primary narcissism and narcissistic self-cathexis – which may be regarded as disordered – all remain unconnected to one another, except that the disordered narcissistic object-choice is linked loosely with 'homosexuals and perverts' and women.*

---

*From Lacan to Kernberg, every analyst does what he wants with the narcissism text, and everyone wants something (very) different; it is seen as one of the most important in the psychoanalytic literature. Freud crammed it full while leaving all of the major points hazy; the text asks to be *read*.

. . . it's all because of you.

I am emphasizing the curious and untypical manner in which Freud's arguments dwindle away because it brings us to two pages in which Freud talks about female love-choice in which he no longer tries to prove anything at all, but simply races along.

The assertions which Freud makes here on female love-choice have often been criticized as demonstrating not only the way he misunderstands women, but also his ignorance or even viciousness. To me they appear (if one reads them as also being aimed strategically) in a somewhat different light; as statements which contain Freud's policy on women *at that moment* (as the drafts for coming moments); sentences which are not so much 'analyses' as pronouncements: which express wishes and expectations regarding women and types of women who were and had been important to Freud and psychoanalysis at that moment and until that moment.

A comparison of the male and female sexes, writes Freud, then shows that there are fundamental differences between them in respect of their type of object-choice, although these differences are of course not universal. Complete object-love of the attachment type is, properly speaking, characteristic of the male.* It displays the marked sexual overvaluation which is doubtless derived from the child's original narcissism and thus corresponds to a transference of that narcissism to the sexual object. This sexual overvaluation is the origin of the peculiar state of being in love, a state suggestive of a neurotic compulsion, which is thus traceable to an impoverishment of the ego as regards libido in favour of the love-object. A different course is followed by the most frequent, probably purest and most authentic type of woman [– three adjectives erected in this one sentence as warning signs before coming to the next]. With the onset of puberty the maturing of the female sexual organs, which up till then have been in a condition of latency, seems to bring about an intensification of the original narcissism, and this is unfavourable to the development of a true object-love with its accompanying sexual overvaluation. Women, especially if they grow up with good looks, develop a certain self-contentment which com-

---

*Just as the concept 'complete object-love' itself obviously introduces a distended penis.

pensates them for the socially elided freedom they have in their choice of object. Strictly speaking, it is only themselves that such women love with an intensity comparable to that of the man's love for them.

Earlier in the text, Freud had accused Jung of simply pronouncing on the libido in the form of decrees. This is not the place to decide who is better at that. But we don't *just* find decrees in Freud's text. In the last sentence but one, for instance, the somewhat elided formulation 'the socially elided freedom they have in their object-choice' touches on the notion that women do not develop 'complete object-love' because they are not even allowed to choose, being rather chosen or traded. The greater 'self-love' of women would in that case be a logical consequence of this social condition; 'narcissism' as protest against forms of marriage in patriarchal society. This socio-critical aside probably contains more truth than the paragraph's psychological speculations.

But Freud is not after *the* truth here. Why does Freud in his psychoanalytic constructions *want* to deny women the complete capacity for loving 'the object'?

They are incapable of sexually overvaluating the object; fine (– one might add: because the men do not wish it; which the polite Freud does not do).

According to Freud they are in love with their own bodies, in the maturing of their hitherto latent sexual organs during puberty; – does he want to say that they are in love with their monthly egg, with their breasts, with the mucous linings that are springing to life in their vaginas? That would be possible were it not for the enforced negative cathexis of menstruation (= wound) in so many girls. (Is there also a commentary on Emma Jung's admission of 'strong autoeroticism' in these sentences? Freud is writing after all about things that happen, about women he *knows*; not just male fantasies, like Weininger* and those guys.)

---

*Otto Weininger (1880–1903): writer of a precocious work entitled *Sex and Character* in which he examined the gulf between the female/maternal and the male/creative. Despite the interest and acclaim he received, he committed suicide shortly after. (Trans.)

But the sentences only first reveal a broader, reasoned sense going beyond mere allusions and conjectures if it is remembered to which women the sentences – in a Freudian text on the female types of loving written in 1914 – were directed: they are (almost exclusively so) the women of the Psychoanalytic Association. And Freud's text proposes certain types of loving to them:

Nor does their need lie in the direction of loving, but of being loved; and the man who fulfils this condition is the one who finds favour with them. The importance of this type of woman for the erotic life of mankind is to be rated very high.

– one senses that Freud at least would rate *this type* of woman very highly. Here Freud is saying (to certain women of the Association) that certain sexual activities are not in their *nature*. A man *finds favour* with them who fulfils certain conditions, i.e. who admires them sufficiently. It is clear that this is not the ideology on which 'normal marriages' are built. Although the sentences do not exactly proclaim a ban on marriage, there is a clear call to the women of the Association not to expect too much from the complete object-love model, were they to have it in mind, and to rely on *being* loved.

For those men and women who are not free of the ineradicable sin of relating the printed word to *themselves*, and who might have felt a certain dissatisfaction with the love relations that such a passage promises, Freud slips a big bonbon:

Such women have the greatest fascination for men, not only for aesthetic reasons, since as a rule they are the most beautiful, but also because of a combination of interesting psychological factors. For it seems very evident that another person's narcissism has a great attraction for those who have renounced part of their own narcissism and are in search of object-love. The charm of a child lies to a great extent in his narcissism, his self-contentment and inaccessibility, just as does the charm of certain animals which seem not to concern themselves about us, such as cats and the large beasts of prey. Indeed, even great criminals and humourists, as they are represented in literature, compel our interest by the narcissistic consistency with which they manage to keep away from their ego anything that would diminish it. It is as if we envied them for maintaining a blissful state of mind – an unassailable libidinal position which we ourselves have since abandoned. The great charm of the narcissistic woman has, however, its reverse side; a large part of the lover's dissatisfaction, of his doubts of the woman's love, of his complaints of her enigmatic nature, has its root in this incongruity between the types of object-choice.

(– in the end the bonbon is slightly poisonous, as fairytale bonbons always are.) The men who belong to beautiful and intellectually developed women (who feel themselves to belong to psycho-analysis) should not expect any special love (particularly not sexual love), but rather put up with a necessary state of dissatisfaction; it will be compensated for by the knowledge of living with an exceptionally beautiful and clever woman, says the text.

In the end that *men love women (object-like) and women themselves (narcissistically)* means, however, *that both* sexes love women, if not in the same way – and that's why things don't work out that well between men and women. I know that Freud does not intend to say this, nor do I know any women who would wish to read him that way: but that is what he *says*.

The first two types of narcissistic object-choice which Freud proposes, (a) loving what one is oneself (oneself) and (b) loving what one was (namely *Her Majesty the Baby* in a previous state of pleasure), can thus be read as formulae both for the women of the Association and for female patients: over-intensive object-love outside of the analysis disrupts the development of transference love.

(The rule of sexual abstinence during 'the cure' rings through these sentences like a sort of ostinato.)

These are sentences to women whom Freud, not ceasing for a moment to be a statesman, needs as daughters in order to build his state; for Freud describes the 'true type' of woman as being none other than the 'young, intelligent, bright, lively, yearning, girl', who is 'like an animal, unaware of her beauty' and positioned unclearly between 'sexual awakening' and matrimony. Basically he is talking about women without men (or women who are only associated with them in a loose, undefined, undecided way, and should as far as possible remain so); he is talking about women for women who are interested in and suited to becoming members of the psychoanalytic state.

Freud provides a programme for two further groups of women, and that in a single paragraph that is added in a manner guaranteed to astonish to the one quoted above:

Even for narcissistic women, whose attitude towards men remains cool, there is a road that leads to complete object-love. In the child which they bear, a part of their own body confronts them like an extraneous object, to which, starting out from their narcissism, they can then give complete object-love.

– a number of authors (e.g. Laplanche and Pontalis) have remarked that such sentences annul the difference that Freud has just introduced between 'narcissistic' cathexis and 'object-love'. That just for the record. More important, with this, Martha (along with other women in her situation) has the consolation of not having been deprived of anything: love for one's children is the wife's complete (narcissistic) love, says Freud. What they may have received from their husbands (or could have given him) would never have matched up to this. In point of fact it may well be true that in many husband/wife relationships the love for the children turns out to be more satisfying than that for the husband. (But does this have anything to do with 'object-choice', with 'narcissism', with the *psychic* realities of the sexes?)

All that is missing now is a bit of love-choice theory for the children themselves, e.g. for one's daughters who will become women; and this is precisely what Freud adds at the end of this paragraph. He requires no more than two sentences for it:

There are other women, again, who do not have to wait for a child in order to take the step in development from (secondary) narcissism to object-love. Before puberty they feel masculine and develop some way

along masculine lines; after this trend has been cut short on their reaching female maturity, they still retain the capacity of longing for a masculine ideal – an ideal which is in fact a survival of the boyish nature that they themselves once possessed.

This is a perfect programme for daughters who do not marry and remain childless, who have identified with a superior father in a masculine way and who (in the most fortunate cases) become the father's successors; just right for the type of daughter which Anna Freud actually became.

Nevertheless, it is doubtful whether Freud had singled out Anna for this task as he wrote these lines; in all likelihood he was thinking more of Anna's older sister Sophie, whom he referred to as his favourite daughter, but she married and died in 1920 of the Spanish flu.

This sort of secretary/aide/successor daughter (as is well known, Freud referred to Anna in this function as his Antigone) is not only restricted to Freud.

In Thomas Mann's diaries 1946–48, which have recently appeared, one can read how glad Thomas Mann was as he watched his daughter Erika ('my favourite child') grow into the roles of secretary, biographer, guardian of his estate, daughter-adjutant.

Daughter-adjutant, a magnificent term. The last section of Freud's 1914 laws on female love-choice is designed for daughters who identify with their father's work.

Turning to the next page in Freud's Collected Works after the *narcissism text* one sees, written in bold letters: MICHAEL-ANGELO'S MOSES. Moses is the figure with whom Freud begins to ally and identify himself in his writing, from now until his death. He presents himself as such in his *narcissism text*, pointing the way through the desert:

Before us stands Herr Freud/Moses with the tablets under his arm (not Herr Blockhead talking nonsense about womanhood).*

---

*Nor King Lear who wanted all the love of all his daughters *just* for himself, and met his ruin.

*

If we turn our gaze away from the world of intentions, strategies and decrees, back to the world of love relationships as they really occur (the less widespread but *more genuine* sort), then the same can be said about 'complete object-love' as was noted for the 'attachment model': it is no rarer among women than men. Indeed, if I'm not mistaken, I have encountered 'complete object-love' (and, moreover, *without sexual overvaluation*) more often among women. (And naturally the women in Freud's Association also loved accordingly.) It is based on a far-reaching understanding of the beloved object's realities (what Emma Jung offered Freud came from this realm). But women who love with a clear gaze are not allowed for, theoretically at least, by Freud (and others). And men not at all (but there are, as we saw, other reasons for that ... related to the procedure of 'free' and 'secret', i.e. concealed, choices. It is not without good reason that the thunderbolt only emits a very *brief* light when it strikes).

Revenants & women in couples, 'without a husband'.

One or two things from the world of love relationships as they really occur should be added here.

In 1933 a strange patient went to Freud for analysis, the American writer Hilda Doolittle, who, as she said, wished to learn more about the links between psychoanalytic and poetic processes than she already knew (I don't believe that anyone knew more about them than her). She presents Freud with a figure, at the same time confirming it anew, that runs through his working and love life like a structural element: the revenant, the female revenant, a leading character in his literary work since the *Interpretation of Dreams.* Freud learned from experience that not only did people from his childhood reappear (in dreams; then outside the dream), but also all the important people in his life had the inherent property of not disappearing from his life once they had entered it; the property of returning in other people, in another form, but clearly, all too clearly as the reappearance of past, abandoned, even forgotten or dead people; a figure whom he named the *revenant*, the one who returns, the never-ending doppelganger of all the important people who had entered his life (life according to the attachment model? A sequence of attachments; good to see in Freud's life).

The first major text that Freud wrote on the relationship between psychoanalysis and literature (1906/7, on Wilhelm Jensen's *Gradiva*) is devoted precisely to this figure, a *female* revenant in this case. (Jung received this text as a present on joining up with psychoanalysis.)

A man, an archeologist (Freud's favourite dream profession), is wandering about the ruins of Pompeii when he meets a woman who hangs in the form of a plaster cast on his wall at home, a woman who had been buried alive 2000 years previously in Pompeii, yet proves to be real; she is not dead, she is alive but also dead. It is the woman from Pompeii (from the plaster cast), but also his childhood sweetheart from the house across the way who had been buried alive in his archeology. Much the same happened on several occasions in Freud's life, in fact so often and so emphatically that during the last 20 years of his life (if not earlier) he was convinced that there were telepathic phenomena which influenced some people so that they inevitably found their way to him 'telepathically'; that everything – this became one of the greatest sources of happiness in his life – would reappear. Nothing is lost if one keeps it alive.

Hilda Doolittle (who wrote under the name H.D.) entered the analysis as a whole bunch of female revenants (as she described in extraordinary detail 20 years later in her book *Tribute to Freud*). She was in contact with a large number of people in psychoanalytic circles, knew all that was to be known at the time coming from or concerning Freud (locked into several information circuits); she mentioned none of this to Freud, playing instead the game of the female revenant in an astonishing manner, so astonishingly that Freud, at once suspicious and entranced, was unable to prevent himself asking her whether perhaps she *prepared* herself for the sessions . . . one wasn't supposed to do that.

For what could she prepare herself? Her history contained a whole series of features that touched on the life (or death) of Freud's daughters Sophie and Anna. I shall mention only two here: on one occasion she must have appeared to Freud as a sort of revenant of his daughter Sophie, who died of the Spanish flu in Hamburg, 1920; at that time 'Spanish flu' was considered incurable. Hilda Doolittle came as a woman who had been infected by the same virus at almost the same time as Sophie, but had overcome the disease (the doctor had given up on her) in a *wondrous* manner. Like Sophie, H.D. had been pregnant and had, shortly before the illness, given birth to a child. H.D. knew that she was bound to strike Freud as the yet-possible impossibility of Sophie's continued existence.

H.D., married but separated from her husband, who was also not the father of her child, had lived since the early twenties in a form of partnership with the English shipowner's daughter Winifried Ellerman, whose nom de plume was *Bryher*. Bryher, childless herself, helped as the second mother or 'father' of the couple to bring up H.D.'s daughter Perdita; she was likewise married but did not live with her husband. The couple appear in an article on H.D. written by Renate Stendhal as 'father-identified daughters' (Freud's type No. 4). H.D., who, like Anna Freud, had worked as her father's secretary, knew that a similar female couple, Anna Freud and Dorothy Burlingham, was living on the floor above the analysis room of Berggasse 19. Dorothy Burlingham was also married, the mother of four children, and separated from her husband. Her children had been Anna Freud's first patients. As the daughter of Louis Comfort Tiffany, writes Paul Roazen, she was easily able to pay for the treatment (even though there were always difficulties with the New Yorkers, who hated 'Jewish' psychoanalysis). (Bryher paid for H.D.'s analysis six months in advance with a 'generous check'.) Bryher herself was undergoing analysis with the Berlin Freudian Hanns Sachs.

Anna Freud and Dorothy Burlingham had become friends while the American woman's children were being treated. Become friends? *They fell in love*; after a certain period of continuing friendship ('engagement period'), Dorothy moved into the Freuds' home in Vienna and stayed.

The appearance of Elisabeth Young-Bruehl's Anna Freud biography allows the type of object-choice involved in the relationship to be defined. Like Anna Freud, Dorothy Burlingham was the youngest child in a series, and, also like Anna, had grown up in a close, tense relationship with her father. As a child, Dorothy Burlingham had felt, as Anna Freud had, like an unwanted hanger-on in her household, a little one who was a bore and a nuisance to the older ones. According to this, a female version of object-choice based on psycho-class.

Freud wrote about the relationship in a letter to Binswanger in 1929:

Our symbiosis with an American family (without a husband), whose children my daughter rears analytically with a firm hand, strengthens more and more, so that even our requirements for the summer are identical . . .

This relationship allows Anna Freud to have children of her own without giving birth or having a husband; produced out of a 'symbiosis' with a suitable daughter from an American family. In his words, Freud saw Anna as having the *paternal* role in the couple. The two also remained together after emigration, and ran the Hampstead Clinic together. Child analysis has *both of them* as mothers.

They were not a lesbian couple, says Young-Bruehl.
A complete transformation of *South of the Border* – sexuality into production sexuality, as with Alma and Alfred Hitchcock? Doubtless that as well, developed from the view that Anna had gained as Sigmund Freud's secretary-daughter (her puberty lasted until her 28th year, says her biographer), a view from the innermost depths of the psychoanalytic office at the more customary forms of object-choice, which was expressed in a letter from Anna to Dorothy in

the formulation: **As far as I can see, being in love is never really enjoyable.**

It wouldn't be wrong to assume that this was Freud's dream relationship (for his own daughters and daughters of his state), Freud's dream couple. (At least after his earlier dream of Anna being united with one of the crown princes turned out to be nothing but Scotch mist.) His well-known animosities towards sons-in-law are not necessarily for personal reasons; in the end they apply to the very fact of *husbands*. When Freud describes himself in a letter to Stefan Zweig in 1936 as blessed with a daughter **who satisfies all of a father's wishes to an extraordinary degree,** he is also including her relationship with Dorothy Burlingham.

Incidentally, the sentence can to some extent be reversed: which father ever left his daughter such a kingdom (field of work, territory in which to live)? And it was *intended* as an inheritance. In the end, Freud's crown prince was a woman. She was linked with the men in the Association (she liked them) as no man could have been: without war. That was more likely to arise with female competitors, such as Melanie Klein. (And with a new King Lacan, whom she avoided after one single contact at a congress.)

Hilda Doolittle on Freud's couch in summer 1933 – she has already seen the swastikas scrawled in chalk on the paving stones that lead to the front door – she comes not only as a messenger from Sophie and as a confirmatory doppelganger of Anna's partner formation, but also as many other figures which I shall not decode here, and as a daughter who shares Freud's dislike of men from the filial genealogy (men from the line of brothers- and sons-in-law); she herself arrives from an alliance with fathers/grand-fathers and, as this special daughter, presents Freud with a special crown, a laurel wreath (at least in her book written in 1956 to commemorate his 100th birthday; whether also conveyed verbally to him in person, I cannot say). With her withdrawal from the many Orpheus-men in her life, particularly D.H. Lawrence, she gives Freud the wreath of the singer, *the* singer who does not injure women, calling him (it had to be an *American* woman for this, one tempered by mythology) Singmund*, him, the 77-year-old with his mouth gnawed away by cancer, who can no longer be approached because of the smell that emanates from the wound – Singmund Orpheus Freud; the one who does not look back on the staircase, who gives at least *some* women a little help on their way up to the Upperworld.

(May the women who have suffered under one or more of the fathers who succeeded him forgive her and myself.) There are still not that many sets of stairs that lead 'outside'; nor is there any real need to bury those that are in the process of being constructed.

* * *

---

*The German word *Mund* means mouth. (Trans.)

Two thoughts by way of conclusion

1. *What is being sung then?*

Something remarkable is being sung, a song that the swallow had not expected to hear as it began to fly around here.

The love-object does not exist, the Freudian procedure seems to be telling us. *Love* is made and sustained by what is virtually a *spectrum* of object-relationships.

In order to lead a life which satisfies his desires regarding both work and love, Freud needs (a) a bride who allows him to draw up a plan for his life and with whose help he can change his personal history; (b) a wife for the children, the home and, for a while, sexual love; (c) a sequence of intellectual women in order to further his own work: working loves or 'medial' women. This sequence is built on, or runs parallel to, another sequence consisting of female patients, with whose help he can gain a certain knowledge and who themselves can change from one sequence to the other; (d) in each of the male production partnerships a central friend, 'crown prince' or 'co-genius'; (e) a daughter-secretary-successor in whose love life a son-in-law-husband does not appear.

These are all aspects of Freud's *love choices*.

The love plateaux that develop in the course of Freud's life ensure that there need be no *separations* from love-objects; there are additions, extensions, displacements (not just *sublimations* – to use Freud's rather unfortunate term). Nor can one find fault with the 80-year-old Freud when he describes his marriage with Martha Bernays as happy. (The people who describe Freud's love life as 'unhappy', because, from a particular moment in time, he no longer slept with Martha Freud, haven't seen much of the Freud film, just the credits.)

All you need, Freud seems to be saying, is to keep the sequences going, to avoid mixing the 5 (perhaps there are even more) sorts of relationships, to avoid making demands on one's wife that she cannot, or will not, fulfil; but to make demands on one's daughter that she can and wants to fulfil; continue, keep on wishing and they will not fail to appear, neither the revenants, nor the moments of love.

The Freudian concept of libido is basically a sequence concept. First the mother is substituted, then the substitutions continue, change levels, unfold. Although *the* love-object does in fact exist (at a point of origin), it is split apart, sub-divided, kaleidoscoped.

Freud himself gives an indication of this in his text on narcissism when he adds this little sentence to the list of possible love objects: **– and the sequence of substitutes who take their place.** Something like that only strikes one (me) with the knowledge of the accompanying story. Previously it looked like a mere appendage.

What is very noticeable in the Freudian procedure is that the separations, the wars, *the divorces* are displaced to a man–man level. The various crown princes leave the analytic state with all the features of divorce-wars; the others, especially the women, remain.

So who or what does '*the libido*' cathect?

– 'in any case only partial objects, never whole persons', as the French Freudians/anti-Freudians have been preaching to the wind for years; and much in Freud accommodates them. Is the libido itself a segmented energy, directed at segments and sequences?

All that stands in the way of this is the thunderbolt, falling helplessly in love, going *all the way* (which, if one takes a closer look at the cases in question, seems, however, to advise: better not to be caught by a *full* blast of libido)

– or, on the other hand, the 'complete object-love' without any misperception, without any sexual overvaluation (in which Freud does not, however, believe; and nor do his critics).

... my life to a rainbow like you.

2. *Where and from what point do women exist?*

The question poses itself because the women whose ways of loving are discussed by Freud all remain within the daughter-genealogy (in one of the cases are daughters who are transformed into mothers). But 'daughters' and 'mothers' are not simply *women*, in the sense that historically there have been (here and there) men who were independent of institutions or states.

All theories of love that have existed till now are concerned with daughters.

The *free-floating* or free-living, free-working woman, independent of institutions or paternal economy, is only now beginning to assume a historical existence (not just as a theoretical possibility, and there are more than just a *handful* of them). And there are already a few more who are independent of paternal *sexuality*.

Faced with the term *woman*, which West-love has plastered over everything that is *up for sale*, usable for *everything* of any conceivable *value* in the encoding system of male-dominated societies, faced with this ubiquitous *WOMAN* it is easy to overlook the fact that women, real individual women, will only actually exist to the degree that they invent themselves as no-longer-daughters. Anna Freud, once independent, was one of them.

Boys will be boys, but girls will be women, according to a sticker that American college women are fond of putting on the doors of their studies. Are they already that far advanced over there?

On the way there (say women psychoanalysts like Luce Irigaray) the daughter status will undergo a transformation: becoming first a daughter-of-the-mother rather than a daughter-of-the-father; a shift in the female psyche (and also in the Freud-state) with unforeseeable consequences. *The Mother–Daughter Plot* is the title of a recent book by Marianne Hirsch which, like many others in America at the moment, points in this direction. Up till now the father-states (including the enlightened Freudian one with partial exits for 'the womenfolk') have presented 'the mother' as a figure that must be rejected by the daughter.

·

. . . law can't touch her at all.

The background to the theory of *penis envy* is the social powerlessness of the mother. *Hole* for vagina is, at a deep-rooted level of being *in the know,* the expression of contempt for the *mother's lack of a phallus,* and by *both* sexes. (Lack of phallus = social powerlessness.)

Freud was not being *completely* unfriendly when he said at least a child would help stopper this hole. (Child = phallus substitute.)

But it is not sufficient help when mothers have to give birth to sons who are programmed to despise them (mother = hole = rubbish pit), and thereafter (attachment model) to despise the women they will marry.

The basic type of (male) attachment-love probably continues to consist in looking for a woman who can be kicked the way one kicked one's mother. The heat build-up of *object-choice* – a conjuring trick for susceptible girls for whom an act is put on. Putting on an act, that's what the man's life consists of.

Attachment without end ... love goes on ... attached to the *atrocities* of the parents, rarely to its nicer side. That is because the wounds in the history of an individual body demand far more treatment than do the more thinly scattered points of beauty.

There are also people who say that *that's* not the reason. People just are that way. Is there a contradiction?

(This section is completely unemphatic ... without love ... breathless.)

*

Until The End Of Time
I'll Be There 4 U
U Know My Heart And Mind
I Truly Adore U.

EPILOGUE ½ *year later (23 years later).*

– the two halves of the globe have fallen into each other's arms, bringing down the walls and shaking the East-bed. There has been

OBJECT-CHOICE and live satellite link-ups as far as life stretches.

Married à la McLuhan (but also a little differently). A lot of people want to give and transmit something to celebrate the new love.

I put on a record, the new one from John Lennon again . . . *I saw a film today, oh boy/The German Army had just won the war.* – Bismarck, says Lennon, is pushing NATO forward to the Oder–Neisse line. *A Day in the Life, 17 July 1990* (the 23rd anniversary of John Coltrane's death, says a voice in my head: *A Love Supreme*).

That is not exactly what East-love, after defecting to a sea of black–red–gold flags, now receives from West-LOVE.

Mutual recognition, says the New York analyst Jessica Benjamin (with Winnicot and other good sounds in her ear), is the prerequisite for enduring object-*relationships*: mutual recognition and acknowledgement of the object's otherness.

Instead of which: the Gordian removal of the Wall by slicing through all differences . . . love caught under the mudguards . . . no mouth prepared to kiss the two halves (introduction of the final kiss of death into the programme).

> where feelings should come into being
> arises the dead sea
> which we show round from morn to night

a poet wrote on 16 February 1990, coolly. What else should he write? That *Money Can't Buy You Love*? No one would believe that.

The Object of Desire (say *BILD** and the TV) is a gold cup, projected onto a vanished wall.

The object of offence has done a vanishing act. On 20 July 1990 it slipped from head to toe into the skin of a so-called Red Army Fraction:**

---

*BILD, the bastion of the yellow press in Germany. (Trans.)

**The date of the attempt by German army officers to assassinate Hitler in 1944 was commemorated after the war in West Germany as 'Resistance Day'. The collapse of the GDR was crowned by the news that the state had harboured RAF terrorists. (Trans.)

... or is this just a confusion.

(– in this way Mr K. will challenge the world.)*

The gate is open, the deep waters have been filled, no halogen searchlights scorching the night, no wicked nun to make the Bundesbank drown, there is nothing left to hinder the longed for embrace of the king's and kaiser's children.** All together now: *All you need is –*

Dissociation and dedifferentiation are the consequences of collapsing old buildings,[†] says psychoanalysis (a doctor not licensed to practise on the Volks-body).

Dissociated (= pure) German feelings approach us ... 40 years of restrained German inner life, roaring for LOVE.

Will it be *love?*

That will probably travel with the last communist (obviously they pick a Jew for *that,* says Andy Rabinach in New York) to the land where the lemons blossom (in *mutual recognition*).[‡]

Probably a very nice place.

We, too, have sat in Arcadia.

END

---

*That is a turning point in history where history is ready to turn.

**The 'Kaiser' is the nick-name of Franz Beckenbauer, manager of the German football team that won the World Cup in 1990. (Trans.)

[†]A play on the name of the notorious and influential industrial music group, Einstürzende Neubauten (= Collapsing New Buildings). (Trans.)

[‡]The last Mohican of German Communism, Gregor Gysi (co-founder of the PDS, the successor party to the East German Communist Party, the SED, is indeed a Jew; 'the land where the lemons blossom' is Goethe's phrase for the happier climes of Italy. (Trans.)

Afterword: Rainbow bridges down the Wandse

The Wandsbek district in Hamburg takes its name from the small river Wandse which winds its way westwards via Eichtal Park to the Holzmühl Pool, through Wandsbek and on, straightened to make the Eilbek Canal, through Eilbek and the Kuhmühl Pool, towards the heart of Hamburg and the River Alster. Rivers, however small, connect everything with everything (*'that's the nature of rivers'*). And this one *connects* the love theorist Freud with the love singers from Liverpool and more besides.

Freud and Martha Bernays studied the sphinx by the Wandse, the Beatles' haircut was invented by the Wandse, the Hamburg Art School, in which Vlado Kristl has his studio and home, lies by the Wandse between these two points, and Martin Langbein also lives by the Wandse, who in the last couple of days took me along a number of paths, four kilometres *down the Wandse*.

No longer living by the Wandse is a sort of person who largely occurs in Germany in the form of memorials, if at all.

One of the three Jewish communities in Greater Hamburg was Wandsbek. Like the second, Altona, until 1864 it lay on Danish and not German territory. After two years under Austrian sovereignty, Wandsbek became Prussian in July 1867, and remained so until 1937; from them on Hamburg-Hanseatic.

During an intermezzo in 1812, the three communities were *one*: Napoleon had amalgamated them. Hamburg was incorporated into the Napoleonic Empire as the 'Département Elbmündung.' (The 'Marseillaise' was sung for the first time in Hamburg on 19 November 1806, on the entry of Napoleon's troops.) The Jewish inhabitants of the *département* received full civic rights; that only lasted a couple of years.

Sigmund Freud and Martha Bernays were married in Wandsbek town hall in Königsstraße. Königsstraße* was named as such because and since the Danish King Christian VIII passed down it in July 1840 as sovereign. Previously it was called 'Neue Koppel'. The marriage in a Prussian town hall (under the swan in the coat of arms of the district of Stormarn, Holstein) would have been quite adequate for a respectable wedding in Wandsbek, but not for Habsburgian Vienna, which in 1886 still sent couples into the churches to be wed. Consequently Freud (who would have been happy to avoid it) and Martha Bernays went to the Wandsbek synagogue (much to the relief of the religious members of the Bernays family).**

The synagogue was just round the corner of Lange Reihe/Königsstraße, a step away from the town hall towards the river. Opposite the spot where the synagogue once stood there is now a bronze plate set into a block of stone. It bears the inscription:

> The synagogue of the former
> Israelite community in Wandsbek
> used to stand on this street,
> previously named Lange Reihe.

---

*Königsstraße = King's Street. (Trans.)
**The invitation reads 'Dr Sigm. Freud/Martha Freud/née Bernays/Married/Wandsbek 14 September 1886. (Trans.)

The House of the Lord was consecrated in 1840:
Its founder was ISAAK HARTWIG (1776–1842).
Previously there had been a prayer room on this street.

Here served as Rabbis:
DR DAVID HANOVER (1833–1901) and
DR SIMON S. BAMBERGER (1871–1961).

On 10 November 1938, during
the nationwide November Pogrom, the police
ensured that the building was not set alight.
Later, however, SA men forced their way in and wrecked it.

The property had to be sold in 1939.
The building was destroyed by wartime bombing in 1943.
RESPECT AT ALL TIMES THE BELIEFS AND THINKING OF OTHERS!
Wandsbek District Council –

– then a date: 1988. On the 50th anniversary of the burning of the synagogues, Hamburg City Council – kissed by the spirit of the place – blessed this text and had it cast in bronze. Now it stands there as testimony to the resistance of the Hamburg police (all old Thälmann* boys) against the rampaging SA men of '38, to changes in the land register in 1939, and to the RAF (Royal Air Force) which was so gracious in 1943.

The inscription spares the local inhabitants who have to pass by (Dotzauer Weg, for pedestrians/cyclists) the word *Jewish*. There is a state 'Israel', and there is also a state called Denmark. In 1988 ff., as a republican district council recalls a *nationwide* November pogram, do any of the passers-by have the feeling as they make their way to the nearby weekly market that it was once Danish/Jewish? The Novembers continue ... the *Houses of the Lord* continue ... in Wandsbek ... Leipzig ... and elsewhere.

---

*Ernst Thälmann (1885–1944): leader of the Communist Party in 1933, who was later executed in a concentration camp. (Trans.)

Wandsbek, like several districts in Hamburg, was largely rebuilt after the 2nd World War, the face of its history shaved clean away, looking as ugly as bombs to this day. The house in which Emmeline Bernays and her daughters lived no longer exists, like all the others, Jewish or non-Jewish, which once stood there. On the site of the Bernays house (at that time Hamburger Straße, now Wandsbeker Marktstr. 38) there is a store, Kaufhalle.

Diagonally opposite, on the other side of the street (across the B 75, a main road), an inscription commemorates the 'Wandsbeker Bote', Matthias Claudius,* who lived there a century earlier. (The chairman of the Jewish community, Beny Beith, also lived there until 1939. *The property had to be sold in 1939.*) To the left of the door, above which is the Claudius inscription, there is now a health food shop. Situated for many years upstairs was the Matthias Claudius Library, a public library that has now moved. To the right, on the ground floor, is a bookshop. On the glass above the entrance (on 1 August 1990) is a blackish-green self-adhesive plastic sign (ugly as bombs) with the words: 'The new Simmel on sale here.'

Matthias Claudius's name is all over Wandsbek, from the chemists to the high school. In 1886 Martha's uncle, the stock-broker Elias Philipp, in whose home Freud spent the last nights before his wedding, lived in Claudiusstraße.

Freud did *not* include Matthias Claudius, the pastor's son, in his Wandsbek genealogy and the plans for his life with Martha Bernays.

But he didn't forget a couple of kings and generals. Freud signed off the first joint letter of the honeymooners Freud/Bernays to Mama in Wandsbek with the lines: **Handed over at our current residence in Lübeck on the first day of the hopefully thirty years' war between Sigm. and Martha.**

Martha was used to such royal phrases, from the start: in one of

---

*Matthias Claudius (1740–1815), pious poet and editor of the newspaper 'The Wandsbek Herald' mentioned here. (Trans.)

the first *letters to his bride,* 7 July 1882, Freud wrote (referring to the rival Wahle): I can afford to be ruthless here. Guai a chi la tocca. That is the oath of war sworn by the Kings of Lombardy at their coronation with the iron crown, and means: *Woe betide him who touches it!* (The Lombard crown turns via Charlemagne into the crown of the *Holy Roman Empire of the German Nation.* Napoleon crowns himself with it in 1805. It is called 'iron' because a nail from Jesus' cross is supposed to have been worked into it.) Not the *tiniest* crown with which Martha's body was so lordly encoded.

Freud could have found others. Rantzaustraße and Tycho Brahe-Weg in Wandsbek testify to another Hamburg–Habsburg connection. Heinrich Rantzau, Danish governor of Schleswig and Holstein (the records describe him as a Medici-like patron of the arts and sciences), bought the estate of Wandsbek in 1564. He brought the Danish astronomer Tycho Brahe to Wandsbek when the latter was driven from his observatory (withdrawal of all income) to an island in the Copenhagen Sound by Christian IV. Tycho Brahe arrived in Wandsbek in 1597 with his family, servants, pupils and several carts packed with instruments and set up his observatory in the castle tower. The first book printed in Wandsbek is (in Latin) Brahe's *Mechanics of the Revised Astronomy,* printed on his own press which he had brought with him.

Brahe had his son take a copy of the book to Emperor Rudolf in Prague, who then appointed him as his court astrologer in 1598. Johannes Kepler collaborated with him in Prague and became his true heir (Brahe, who entered posterity with the title the 'King of Astronomers', was already dead in 1601). Since 1984, Kepler and Brahe have had a joint memorial in Prague. Never again have so many letters from princes and scholars passed to and from Wandsbek as in that year [1598], writes Wilhelm Grabke in *Wandsbek und Umgebung* [Wandsbek and Vicinity] (Hamburg 1960), completely forgetting the scholar Freud who in 1960 was not a king in the annals of Wandsbek's scholars.

This at any rate was the first Habsburg–Wandsbek connection.

Christian IV, who expelled Tycho Brahe, was also the founder of the small town of Glückstadt, forty kilometres to the north of Hamburg down the river Elbe. A Danish port was to arise there, closer to the sea, as competition for mighty Hamburg and as a customs barrier. (In 1630 a naval battle was fought on the southern Elbe over the tobacco duty that Christian IV levied on the Hamburg ships.) I lived in Glückstadt for three years from 1956 in no. 12 Christian IV. Straße, not knowing a thing about *Christian Four*, as we called him, or about Tycho Brahe or Rudolf, with only the American King in my ear. I first came across the name and a portrait of Tycho Brahe on the cover of SUN RA's *Heliocentric Worlds*. SUN RA, discoverer of new galaxies in black music.

Next door to the Bernays' house in Wandsbek was an inn, the 'Harmonie'. The first anti-semitic assembly was held there in November 1891, writes Astrid Louven in *Die Juden in Wandsbek (1604–1940), Spuren der Erinnerung*, [The Jews in Wandsbek, 1604–1940, Clues to Remembrance] (Hamburg 1989), published in an edition of 500 numbered copies. The assembly of 600 people demanded that equal rights for Jewish citizens be abolished and that 'foreign Jews' should be banned from immigrating to Wandsbek (according to the police report).

Immediately after the 2nd World War the Kino Harmonie, one of Hamburg's largest cinemas at the time, was erected on the site of the Bernays' house and the likewise bombed inn. On the other side of the street another cinema rose similarly from the ruins, the Rex. Martin Langbein had often sat in the Arcadia of the Harmonie or of the Rex opposite, (now discovering that Martha Bernays had received Freud's letters, as well as Freud himself, on the spot where the mail from American Westerns and pirate films reached the young Hamburg cinema fans who watched the Sunday children's matinees in the fifties. The two cinemas have also disappeared since then; replaced by stores, as has been mentioned).

Before May 1898 there were five further anti-semitic meetings in the 'Harmonie', even though (or because) there were fewer and fewer Jews among the inhabitants of Wandsbek. The Jewish community had declined in importance with the amalgamation of all the Hamburg communities; many of the Wandsbek Jews moved to other locations, including Walter A. Berendsohn (who left the Matthias Claudius high school in 1899), one of the first academic authors in Germany to write books on Hamsun. Later, in Sweden, he also set up the first institute for exile research. Others tried to assimilate themselves to the Germans; in 1900 there were only seven children left in the Jewish school, which 'closed down in 1901' (Grabke).

On 9 November 1913 the rabbi, Dr Bamberger, and the chairman of the Jewish community, Benny Beith, call on the Lord Mayor of Wandsbek, Wasa Rodig, who on 10 November sends a letter to Headmaster Peterson of the Matthias Claudius high school, saying: The Jewish community is of the opinion that the teaching staff at the high school has aspired to make the school free of Jews, and has now succeeded in doing so ...

It can be assumed that the phrase *free of Jews* did not come from Bamberger and Beith. Headmaster Petersen, by return of post: complaints about the *administration of his office* should be addressed to the superior authorities ... what else.

All that can be *seen* today of the one-time Jewish life in Wandsbek is (apart from the memorial stones) the Jewish cemetery. Trespassers are kept out by tall iron railings, and it is overgrown by pine trees whose branches brush the graves, a paradise for bumble bees amidst the roar of the cars around it.

One can peer through the railings and make out the Hebrew inscriptions on the gravestones. The railings do for the graves what the police did for the synagogue in November 1938.

There are a number of other aspects of Wandsbek history that are worth mentioning, such as the blossoming contraband trade in tobacco in the 1880s, when Freud walked about it (Wandsbek had for a long time been a duty free area; tobacco workers were one of the largest occupational groups in Wandsbek), a convenient area for a cigar-freak like Freud (until a short while ago there was a branch factory of the Reemtsma tobacco company by the Wandse).

Lastly just a word on the man who gave his name to Nebendahlstraße in Wandsbek: Nebendahl was a municipal architect of Wandsbek who also invented the remote ignition device for gas lamps. It allowed all of the street's lamps to be lit at one go, an act which reminded Freud in a letter to O. Pfister, dated 8 November 1934, of the first miracle of creation of psychoanalysis and its 'let there be light!' Nebendahl for the outer, Moses Freud for *The Inner Light*.

George Harrison, who penned the Beatles' version of 'The Inner Light', was the second member of the band to receive the Beatles haircut in Hamburg. The first was Stuart Sutcliffe, who shortly after left the band to enrol as a student at the Hamburg School of Art – a good two kilometres down the Wandse from the Wandsbek of Freud/Bernays. John Lennon, already friends with Sutcliffe at the art school in Liverpool, hoped to change Sutcliffe's mind during the Beatles' 4th engagement in Hamburg in 1963 and bring him back to the group. Stu Sutcliffe was *in love* with a student at the Hamburg School for Fashion and Design (a kilometre further along the Wandse in the direction of Hamburg city centre), Astrid Kirchherr. The Beatles chronicles present her as the inventor of the Beatle cut; first Sutcliffe and Harrison, then the rest of the group.

In November 1960, only two months after their first meeting, Stu and Astrid got engaged. They put their money together and went out and bought the rings – one for each of them, in the German fashion. Then they drove in her car along the Elbe.

The Beatles didn't have a car in 1960.

The first professional photographs of the most photographed faces of the 20th century also came from Astrid Kirchherr. Her fiancé, Stu Sutcliffe, died in 1962 in Hamburg of the after-effects of a brawl in Liverpool.

Klaus Voormann, also a student at the School for Fashion and

Design (bass player on a number of Lennon's later recordings and friend of Astrid Kirchherr; he 'discovered' the *Beatles* in the '*Kaiserkeller*' on the Reeperbahn), did the cover for *Revolver* in 1966, the first LP cover by a German to win a Grammy Award.

Without going out of my door/I can know all things on earth, sings George Harrison in 'The Inner Light'. That is another sort of knowledge.

I've reached the end of this walk along the river, Mundsburg subway station, Uhlenhorst, shortly before the Elbe Canal opens into the outer reaches of the Alster.

Back at the starting point, not five kilometres up the Wandse, there are two stone sphinxes standing at the entry to Eichtal Park, quite finely carved on two not so fine rectangular brick bases. One can take a look at them now. They once belonged to Count Schimmelmann (who has all of three streets named after him in Wandsbek) and stood in front of his Hamburg town house: they were carved in sandstone around 1775 by Johann Wilhelm Manstaedt. In Freud/Bernays' time the palace had been turned into an inn. The landlord wanted to get rid of the sphinxes so he gave them to the Wandsbek leather manufacturer Caspar Oskar Luetgens, who in turn had them placed on a bridge over the Wandse in a park he created. Freud's first visit to Wandsbek coincided with the arrival of the two stone figures on the bridge.

Let's *assume* they went there; then the sphinx which stretches itself in this book is one of the two which King Oedipus (King Lackland) and his bride passed when, in 1882 ff., they crossed the river. And one stops on bridges (muses on *sphinx figures*, whose notorious mysteriousness, insofar as they are woman, consists of the efforts of men to hide just how *little* mystery their dealings with women, insofar as they are not sphinx, contain).

From the sphinxes to lost Jewish corners to *Revolver* and 'Tomorrow Never Knows', an arc spanning two engagements, 1882/1960, invisible *Rainbow Bridge* from psychoanalysis to Mersey Beat *down the Wandse*, and in the middle of the arc Vlado Kristl, now painting and writing in Blumenau; 'on the way' a story of obliterations, not *visible* when one goes there, and scarcely 'knowable'.

It was known (or rather discovered) by Martin Langbein, inhabitant of Eilenau (where we lodge when we pass through Hamburg) which runs parallel to the left bank of the Wandse. Thanks to a grant from the Jan Philipp Reemtsma Foundation, Martin Langbein can for now make himself, with his ever-branching researches and translations for the *Book of Kings*, a paid collaborator. Many thanks from here on to JPR (we don't know each other personally).

*

From Heinrich Heine, whom Freud frequently quotes from the *Interpretation of Dreams* onwards, but whom, writing to Martha, he did not include explicitly in the line of predecessors (perhaps because it was *all too* evident that he was a part of it: Ludwig Bernays, related to Isaac Bernays, was friends with Heine and printed poems by him in the émigré newspaper *Vorwärts!* which he published in Paris; in addition, Mary, the second wife of Elias Philipp, with whom Freud spent the nights before his wedding, was a Heine by birth; the two had a daughter Martha, born 1882). On the last occasion that Heine was in Wandsbek before going to Paris in 1831, he wrote the following love song (*object-choice 'Rose'*):

> Softly singing measures wind
> Sweetly through my mind.
> Ring, little song of spring,
> Ring out unconfined!
>
> Ring far out, where blossoms sprout
> Round a house you'll see.
> If you find a rose about
> Say hello for me.

My singing mother-radio included this as part of its morning repertoire: flickering heath-air in the kitchen; the cooking held its breath, just as I held it once more on hearing Marlene Dietrich sing the words in a Sternberg film (it was also sung for a young boy on a hay cart who was '*fleeing* from the invaders'*). Flight from a man whom she loved and who loved her, flight to a life of her own as a singer, as show-woman *White Lady* in a King Kong costume with removable hairy gloves, Ellington-like growls in his horns (there was always a bit of the Wandsbek chimes in the *Roses*). It took my breath away and left me with this highly charged speechlessness, this inability to speak when beset by strong feelings, which reminds me that *Love* (or is it an *idea* of love) is located, among other places, in one of the two spots in *his* body which Freud describes as the seat of the phenomenon of *repression*: in the throat. (The second, for Freud, was the lower opening of the body.) This touches on the love-*forms* in which one loves: loving either the chosen object or other people. That is something different to the choice *of the object* which was being considered here (and will be on another occasion).

> If you find a rose about, say nevertheless . . .

– and:

> I'd like to thank the man who wrote the song
> That made my baby fall in love with me.

---

*Namely the author, who fled from East Prussia at the end of the Second World War. (Trans.)

Printed in the United States
by Baker & Taylor Publisher Services